I0797058

ULTIMATE QUESTIONS

ULTIMATE QUESTIONS

A STAKEHOLDER GUIDE TO THE BUSINESS OF YOUR LIFE

ANDREW C. WICKS

with Alexander S. Bleiberg and John K. Nolan

DARDEN BUSINESS BOOKS

University of Virginia Press

Charlottesville and London

The University of Virginia Press is situated on the traditional lands of the Monacan Nation, and the Commonwealth of Virginia was and is home to many other Indigenous people. We pay our respect to all of them, past and present. We also honor the enslaved African and African American people who built the University of Virginia, and we recognize their descendants. We commit to fostering voices from these communities through our publications and to deepening our collective understanding of their histories and contributions.

DARDEN BUSINESS BOOKS
an imprint of the University of Virginia Press

Printed in the United States of America on acid-free paper

First published 2025

1 3 5 7 9 8 6 4 2

ISBN 978-0-8139-5426-4 (hardback)
ISBN 978-0-8139-5428-8 (ebook)

Library of Congress Cataloging-in-Publication Data
is available for this title.

Epigraph on page ix from "Little Gidding," from *The Complete Poems and Plays, 1909–1950* by T. S. Eliot. Copyright 1950, 1943, 1939, 1930 by T. S. Eliot. Copyright 1952, 1936, 1935 by Harcourt Brace & Company. Copyright renewed 1964, 1963, 1958 by T. S. Eliot. Copyright renewed 1980, 1978, 1971, 1967 by Esme Valerie Eliot. Used by permission of HarperCollins Publishers.

Mount Sopris image adapted by Leigh Ayers
from photograph by Andrew C. Wicks.

COVER AND BOOK DESIGN BY LEIGH AYERS

To my students

CONTENTS

PREFACE

We shall not cease from exploration
And the end of all our exploring
Will be to arrive where we started
And know the place for the first time.
—**T. S. ELIOT**, "Little Gidding," *Four Quartets*

Part of me is frustrated that it took me so long to come up with the idea for Ultimate Questions—both as a class and as a book. I'm in the latter stages of my career as a business ethics professor, and it would have been so much nicer to have figured this out earlier so I could build on and develop the ideas to their fullest potential. And maybe because I started the class so late, it's taken quite some time to develop the book: a full eight years from the first outline (which came to me like a bolt of lightning, on a beach in Hawaii, where my wife, Cathy, and I were celebrating our ten-year anniversary) to a version that feels right is not what I'd planned on or hoped for. A clear factor in this process is that this is a new kind of writing for me. I'm not used to writing for a general audience about how to embed deep questions in our everyday lives. There are many ways to write a book of this kind, and most of them are not what I wanted to do. It has taken many false starts and bad drafts to find the way to this version.

Yet as I reflect now, I realize that I'm writing the book at just the right time. It is all coming together as I move into the final phases of my work life and, at the same time, face my own health challenges and mortality. I have been going through an odyssey of sorts for the last seven to eight years. I have a neurodegenerative disease. It began gradually and was very hard to notice for the first few years, yet now it dramatically impacts my daily life. How clear (or foggy) I am mentally affects my energy, relationships, teaching—most everything I do.

Cathy noticed these changes first and began advocating for me. She has been helping me to grasp some of what is going on; she's put a health care team together; and we are slowly finding our way. It has taken several years to navigate this—we had to change and adapt our medical support, and we struggled to align our lived experience with what medicine is able to diagnose. We sought medical advice and heard a great deal of "nothing to see here" from many people in the medical world who, to our great surprise, didn't seem to want to acknowledge or name what was going on. We are grateful to have made some real progress in ruling some things in and other things out, but throughout the entire process, we have had to struggle with great uncertainty. We are now working with some of the best neurologists in the world, and we have clear evidence that there is a biological basis for these changes. I have a diagnosis that puts this strange and disorienting period of my life into some perspective, even as more is going on than has yet been named.

As we have built a health care team, we have also moved back to Colorado, where I grew up. While our home was in Aurora, we also had a small and simple cabin, set on five acres of land at the foot of Electric Peak amid the Rockies. As a child, I would sit and stare at those mountains for long stretches—they had a kind of presence for me that brought awe and joy. Seeing them filled an ache inside of me that I didn't know existed. In her wisdom, Cathy brought us both back to our first and last Colorado home together. After much exploration, we have come back to the beginning. All our experiences have brought challenges and tests,

Mount Sopris, Colorado

but also beauty and play. It is hard to know a place if you stay only there, and coming back to these mountains, I see them (and myself) with new eyes. T. S. Eliot conveys this feeling beautifully in "Little Gidding" (*Four Quartets*), a poem that both Cathy and I find deeply moving and so fitting for this last chapter of our lives. The mountains all around both comfort me and bring me the same wonder I felt as a child. And as I live with this ever-changing illness, the mountains remind me of striving to be my best, to accomplish hard things, to feel the discomfort of facing my fears and the joy of reaching the peak—as well as the descent that clarifies the learning.

We all face hardship. We all know about uncertainty, fear, and struggle; we've all experienced, or will experience, disease, divorce, disruptions, and death. Even a relatively "normal" life has plenty of moments that disorient us, throw into question many of the most basic assumptions we make about the world, and cause fear and deep anxiety. I share a bit of my story simply to tell you that part of what has prepared me to write this version of the book is my own journey, which has forced me to wrestle with these ultimate questions in ways that are deeply personal and far from an academic exercise. Even as I look out my window at beautiful Mount Sopris, I am also staring squarely at my own mortality. I am losing perspective on the person I used to be (even the "me" of six months ago), and my whole world is shrinking. This journey that I'm on has pushed me to live the questions I pose in this book in a new and more urgent way. They have been a very explicit part of my everyday life: I wonder each day what my body and my mind will be able to give me, where I will falter, what I won't be able to do that I once did with ease. I lament how my decline is diminishing my ability to help my students, colleagues, family, and friends. As these changes happen, I find new ways to pivot and improvise. I have found myself seeking new ways to adapt, just to get through the day and avoid being "discovered" by people who don't know there is anything wrong with me. In one of Cathy's favorite stories about how I adapted, I went to the grocery store and came home without several things we'd agreed I should buy. I tried to say, as casually as I could, "They were out of that." After the first few times this happened, she caught on and called me on it—with empathy and grace—which helped me get beyond the shame I felt for not being able to do something so basic. Now we can have a good laugh about it. Indeed, some of the adaptations I have made (both consciously and unconsciously) have led to the funniest moments of our marriage—we found ways to turn potential shame and division into shared laughter and a closer connection. It has helped immensely to be with a partner who is so patient and who wants to be with me as I go through this process. Our approach definitely beats just being sad and angry at these changes and how they have forced us to adapt. While there have been plenty of moments where we got stuck in the sadness and anger, together we have found a way to hold the tension of joy and suffering and find our own "third way" through it.

At times, though, this process has been overwhelming. I have shed more tears in the last two years than I had in my entire life before this—crying fits come over me like waves and can last for thirty minutes or more. Turns out these fits of uncontrollable sadness are part of the disease process. In such moments, we have many options for how to respond. We can try to not acknowledge this uncomfortable reality, as many friends and family members have done, and act like everything is fine. While this reaction has been frustrating to deal with and can make me feel isolated, I can understand why they continue to want to see me as "just fine." Nobody wants to face what is going on, and trying to see how much I'm still "me" makes it far more convenient to get through the day. We can deny reality (either consciously or unconsciously), or we can do our best to wake up and see what is happening, even when it is painful. I came to see the questions in this book as an invaluable tool for reclaiming my own agency in how I meet my circumstances and what I make of these changes—changes that are coming more rapidly and invasively each day. The questions have, quite honestly, been vital to my ability to wake up with a sense of hope and purpose every day. This work has been one of the most helpful things I have found in this process: The passion I feel to write about the questions helps keep me going, and at the same time, contemplating them helps me remain grounded and see that I have as much work to do as anyone who reads this book.

So, even as I'm asking you to go on this journey, I want you to know it is a journey I have been on for quite some time. I have been asking versions of the four ultimate questions for most of my life, sometimes without fully realizing it. It is just part of how I'm wired; it is why I went to graduate school and why I have loved life as a professor who asks "big questions" with my feet on the ground, trying to figure out the best path through life. Yet I have been even more conscious of these questions over the past seven to eight years and more aware of how they show up in my life each day. Climbing my beloved Rockies requires paying attention, noticing things we have been trained to ignore, getting out of our comfort zones, working hard, and facing fears. Mount Sopris, which delights me every time I look out my window, is not just a warm and fuzzy view. It is a beautiful, powerful metaphor for living with ultimate questions. And like any child gazing up at a mountain, I do not pretend that I bring any special skill or insight to this work—other than to help you see that these questions are everywhere and that life is better when we take care to recognize them and decide how to respond. Like a novice hiker navigating a steep path, considering the questions with intentionality and clarity helps us to see what is at stake, to find new paths, places where we can grow and find meaning, to make sense of our lives. We can use these ultimate questions to make sure we are awake and aware, so that we can more fully embrace the odyssey of our journey through life. That is the opportunity offered in this book. I hope it is one that you will welcome as a chance to think deeply about yourself and your life while also using these questions and exercises as a practical set of tools. They remind us that as we inevitably have to act and make choices, those choices are better when we see what is at stake and when we keep in mind what is important to us. In short, this book is not just the idle musings of a philosopher—it is an effort to bring about more wisdom, intention, and reflection so that we can live more of the life we seek rather than feeling like victims of forces working against us.

We face these questions every day—it is better to do so when we can see the questions, wrestle with them, and choose to live them intentionally and in the best way available to us.

— Andy Wicks, March 2025

INTRODUCTION

The unexamined life is not worth living.
—**SOCRATES**

Have patience with everything unresolved in your heart and . . . try to love the questions themselves as if they were locked rooms or books written in a very foreign language. Don't search for the answers, . . . because you would not be able to live them. And the point is, to live everything. Live the questions now. Perhaps then, someday far in the future, you will gradually, without even noticing it, live your way into the answer.
—**RAINER MARIA RILKE**, *Letters to a Young Poet*

Imagine . . . You are sitting poolside on a warm summer afternoon when you casually glance up and notice someone across the pool. The shape of the day changes as you see this person, some force in you overpowers your natural shyness, and you find yourself approaching them, introducing yourself, and easing into a conversation. Within a few months you start dating. You have been burned before in a long-term relationship and are a bit gun-shy, but that deeper sense of something special going on allows you to believe that maybe this time is different.

Or . . . You have just graduated from business school and are struggling with what to do. Many of your fears about the long hours and the hard edge of consulting turned out to be true—and the job offer you've received is much less appealing than what you'd hoped for. Still, given your substantial college debt and your desire to build financial stability, this consulting position seems like the best option. Perhaps you will learn to like it. The other option on the table is a last-minute opportunity to be the executive director for a local nonprofit whose mission you believe in. The pay you'd make is a small fraction of what you'd earn in consulting, yet the title and the quality of the work are very enticing. The clock is ticking, and you need to make a decision.

Or . . . You hear from your mother that her latest health checkup didn't go as planned. The pain she was feeling in her stomach wasn't just a sign of aging or stress, as you'd suspected, but a symptom of the cancer that has been metastasizing in her body for months. The only possible decision now is between options for palliative care. You can't imagine life without your mother, or who you will be if she isn't there to be a part of it.

Moments like these remind us that there are larger questions at play that guide us even when we aren't consciously thinking about them, caught up as we so often are in the minutiae of our daily lives.

"ULTIMATE QUESTIONS AND CREATING VALUE FOR STAKEHOLDERS": THE CLASS

About a decade ago, I made what felt like an audacious choice to create a course called "Ultimate Questions and Creating Value for Stakeholders." At the time, I didn't know what to expect. I had been at the University of Virginia's Darden School of Business for about a decade by then, teaching a required first-year business ethics class along with the odd elective or executive education seminar. Given the reception of that class, and a smattering of teaching awards and other recognition, I felt confident that at least some students would show up, if only for the sake of taking another class with me. But when enrollment opened for the new course, I wasn't sure if the name of the course would prove daunting and scare away everyone other than a die-hard core group of students.

The response surprised me. During the first two years, enrollment barely fit under the forty-person cap that I had implemented to ensure students could build strong connections during the course. And by the third year, enrollment for the class had soared. As it turned out, students didn't need to be persuaded to reflect on the deep questions of life. Instead, they sought out those opportunities, even when it meant losing the chance to take other classes that were more directly applicable to their jobs.

The experience of teaching the class was equally surprising. I had half expected to need to push students to really go deep. I had thought they would need pressure from me to wade beyond the "kiddie pool" of nonchallenging conversations and to be honest and vulnerable about the most profound aspects of their identities, values, and beliefs. These conversations are difficult and can even be risky, especially when they touch on topics like politics and involve people who think quite differently from each other. They require opening ourselves to the possibility of not only disagreement and challenge, but also judgment, disapproval, and exclusion. When we disclose the deepest aspects of ourselves, we shed the armor of concealment that protects us. I was asking a lot of my students, and I wasn't sure they'd be willing to go where the questions (and I) wanted to take them—out of the safe space of having their views supported and validated and into discussions with people who disagreed with them. But in their classroom conversations, presentations, and small-group activities, my students did incredible things. Every class (and every student) was different, and some were more willing to dig in than others, but their efforts as a group left me consistently impressed. They were getting there on their own. All they needed was a space to do so, and perhaps, occasionally, a gentle nudge from me.

They taught me as well. Like every other Darden professor, I teach using the case method, which puts a premium on professors asking questions of students rather than repeating what is in a textbook or handing out "answers." Instructors are more like conductors of an orchestra, trying to get the best out of each participant and helping the students to work together and to learn actively through a process of discovery that *they* lead. "Ultimate Questions" fits perfectly in this model of instruction, and during my years of teaching it, I've learned from my students what works and what doesn't. The insights are broadly applicable—I recommend them to friends, parents, mentors, managers, people in the larger community (in other words, everyone)—and I've compiled them in an appendix at the back of this book called "A Guide to Having Hard Conversations."

My students are generally in their late twenties to late thirties (though when I teach in the Executive MBA program, they tend to be significantly older); they've had some work experience; and they're at Darden to learn the skills and make the connections they need to be successful in the business world. After graduation, they go on to start their own businesses, consult for major firms, manage multinational corporations, and guide innovations in tech, human resources, sustainability, and more.

Which leads me to the second part of my course name: "Creating Value for Stakeholders." I see this course as not just about our own personal, private ways of understanding the world, but also about how our views on ultimate questions relate to what we do with others, including what goes on at work. I push my students to see that business is necessarily entangled in the activity of ultimate questions—and that while parts of that are scary (for example, if companies are shaping how we think about these questions in ways we aren't aware of), this is a good thing. Considering ultimate questions in the world of business offers the opportunity to deepen our understanding of these questions and see why paying attention to them matters so much.

While there are many ways to understand business, our society (and much of the world) has adopted an understanding of business that emphasizes profit—meaning individual self-interest and the primacy of shareholders. Some scholars have introduced ideas about the physics of money, an allegedly scientific, objective understanding of factors that cause wealth to increase or decrease, money to be made or lost.

This way of thinking has been driven by many forces, but especially by a major change in economics.[1] Before the eighteenth century, economics and ethics were largely interrelated. With the Enlightenment, the focus shifted to scientific objectivity and experiment, which had the unfortunate result in economics of eroding and then largely removing the complexity (and messiness) of humans—which includes, of course, ethical concerns and dilemmas. Humans were simplified into self-interested actors, and that was that. As part of the same shift, economists began talking about business in ways that put mathematics and statistics at the forefront. This was partly related to their efforts to get a seat at the table of influence in public policy, to grow their academic prestige, and to suggest that their discourse was more factually "real" and rigorous—rather than just academic arguments among competing theories of business. Many modern economists like to see themselves as objective observers of a rule-based system driven by abstract notions of profit and shareholder value.[2]

This new focus on self-interest implies that business owners have only one real motive: profit. As businesspeople, we might say we care about others and want to improve society, limit pollution, or support social justice—but in fact these goals are just window dressing to try to make us feel better. All that really matters is money and self-interest. Such single-minded thinking is not only bad psychology; it also leads us to approach business in a way that enshrines selfishness (meaning we feel obliged to act more selfishly than we would otherwise).

The assumption that people act from just one motive—self-interest—is both odd and optional. In our private lives, we have no trouble with people being motivated by a variety of factors and not just one thing. We have our individual interests, yet we also care about others—our community, our family, and our friends. And even within our own interests, we may find a variety of things we value, many of which are in conflict. This focus on profit and profit alone doesn't reflect how humans think and operate most of the time, and in fact it leads us to embrace a way of living, talking, and acting that emphasizes money and greed—and makes a joke of "business ethics" (and, yes, I have heard most of the one-liners out there about why *business ethics* is an oxymoron). If we rig the game to say humans can only care about one thing and that has to be our own interest (which, in business, means making as much money as possible), we shouldn't be surprised to see people advocating views of business that glorify greed. And this way of thinking has similar effects beyond our strictly business dealings—scientists have found that students of economics, accounting, and commerce are more likely to focus on themselves than others, to the extent of choosing, at much higher rates than others, to betray their partner in a prisoner's dilemma game or to make more one-sided offers in ultimatum games.[3] Starting from these premises shapes our behavior and that of others in ways that tend to make those premises and predictions self-fulfilling.

By contrast, before this turn toward "objectivity" and self-interest, many of the great founding economists were also moral philosophers. They saw economics as one aspect of living a moral life and being fully human. Even Adam Smith, author of *The Wealth of Nations*, perhaps the most important book to usher in modern capitalism, considered his best book *The Theory of Moral Sentiments*—which begins by explicitly rejecting selfishness as the only motivator: "How selfish soever man may be supposed, there are evidently some principles in his nature, which interest him in the fortune of others, and render their happiness necessary to him, though he derives nothing from it except the pleasure of seeing it."[4] Smith highlights *sympathy* as the foundation of morality and of all life in community, and this focus implies a few noteworthy things about business that we seem to have forgotten: The job of businesspeople is to find ways to do things for others to make them better off. You get paid by a customer because you have done something that merits their giving you their money in proportion to the value you created. Yes, you should do well financially in that transaction, yet the pathway to doing well is recognizing the interest of the other party and actively advancing it. The business world is not an abstract reality to be analyzed, but a living, breathing ecosystem that is actively shaped by individual humans discussing and participating in it.

In short, when we focus on the interests of others, it becomes easier to see business as a moral activity and a vehicle for improving society. It is about both "self" and "other" at the same time; efforts to pull them apart and focus on just one miss the mark.

My colleagues and I have worked hard to reclaim Adam Smith's idea that business is about people coming together to make each other better off—to create new products and services that customers want to buy, to offer jobs that employees want to do and that can grow their capabilities, to help suppliers get better and build their operations, and to provide returns and benefits that lead shareholders to want to own stock and communities to want to have those businesses in their towns. Practiced this way, business is the kind of thing everyone should want around.

This alternative way of thinking about business was most eloquently expressed by my colleague Ed Freeman as *stakeholder theory*.[5] It advocates that businesses focus on serving stakeholders who make the firm a viable and ongoing entity—and stakeholders can include, for example, customers, suppliers, employees, financiers, and members of the local community. If we focus on taking care of these people and learning what they want from their interaction with the company, then we have the makings of a great business.

In this view, business is not defined by the soul-crushing, obsessive focus on profits that leads a business owner to see people only as a means to a profitable end. Even laying out the logic of this "business" view sounds oppressive and antihuman. It also leads proponents of this approach into some very awkward situations. One of my favorites is an expression that many of my students have heard from their bosses: "Our people are our most important assets." When I ask my students, "Who has heard this from your company leadership?," about 70 percent of the hands in the room go up. When I follow up with "How many of you believe that is true?," about 75 percent of the hands that were raised go down.

What does it mean to take care of people at work? How can the company demonstrate that? What do employees want and expect from company leaders in order to believe it when they say, "Our people are our most important assets"?

Without thoughtfulness, open-mindedness, and commitment to follow through, empty promises and platitudes only reinforce stereotypes of business as heartless, amoral, and psychopathic. They reveal management as disingenuous and imply that stakeholders should actively distrust what they say, which in turn reduces management's ability to get people to collaborate, trust each other, and do their best for the company.

In the alternative my colleagues and I have laid out, business starts with humans, with face-to-face interactions, with businesspeople motivated by a desire to actively take care of others while also caring about themselves and their interests. When a great team of stakeholders collaborates to make each other better off, good things tend to happen. People feel valued and seen, and they want to continue to be part of an organization because they see and experience how it serves their interests.[6] And the organization tends to do well because it is built and staffed by people who are motivated and who want to work for a firm that advances their interests and contributes to making people better off. This account still says that the "money matters"—but instead of morality being a separate, inauthentic part of a business's self-justification, it is a core aspect of responsible leadership in business. Firms care about the money because they have a moral responsibility to do so—not just for their shareholders, but also because customers want great, affordable products; employees want quality, high-paying jobs; suppliers want to benefit from working with the business; and the community wants the resources that come from the firm being there. All these groups want the business to care about serving them—and caring about the money (but not *just* about the money) is part of how managers show they care about their stakeholders. The more that managers understand their stakeholders and what they want, especially as that evolves and changes over time, the better off they will be in operating and growing their business for both the short and the long term.

Taking this view requires that we give up the desire to neatly separate the ethics part from the self-interest part of how we understand people and what happens in markets. Even though doing so complicates efforts to generate theories and predictions that are rigorous and systematic, it helps us gain a better understanding of humans, as well as develop a better kind of language and framework for how we think about business. Ideas matter, and having lopsided and overly simplistic views results not only in bad theories but also in self-fulfilling narratives where people feel obliged to act more in line with those theories.

To understand our stakeholders—simply to understand *each other*—we need to cultivate what Adam Smith understood as sympathy: the ability to engage with and imaginatively adopt the perspectives of others. And part of this involves recognizing our own perspectives. Happily, we can do both at the same time. We can get better acquainted with ourselves and forge deeper connections with others by talking with each other about what really matters: the deep questions that guide our lives.

It was gratifying to see my students make these connections and appreciate the importance of talking about these ideas—not just for their individual views about the world, but because they are leaders who shape what happens in their businesses. After a few years, the demand for my "Ultimate Questions" class greatly exceeded capacity. I started to receive more and more requests for accommodation from students who hadn't been admitted into the course. I could tell that these students desperately wanted a space to wrestle with these questions, both on their own and in conversations with their peers. I could sense their eagerness, their hunger for this opportunity. But I also knew that the course would lose some of its specialness if I tried to accommodate everyone. I knew that the rich connections between students would become harder to sustain if the class became larger. I knew I had to keep the course capped, but I started to feel guilty about the students I wasn't admitting, as though I was denying them something they needed and were entitled to—as well as something I wanted to give them. We all deserve this opportunity for deep, conscious reflection about the most important questions of life, whether or not we attend the Darden School of Business at the University of Virginia. These reflections led me to the idea of writing this book.

The challenges of turning a class experience into a book are obvious. Those challenges were especially acute in this case. Classrooms provide a setting in which to wrestle with a topic as a (relatively small) group. That setting has proved especially fruitful in the case of "Ultimate Questions," because it's through the sometimes-rough elbowing of conversation about deep topics with trusted peers that our own beliefs become clarified and we can feel truly seen. Talking about these questions in real time creates moments where people feel quite vulnerable, which can lead to feelings of rejection or being misunderstood as well as profound acceptance and empathy. That kind of experience can't be replicated in a book. But my hope is that this book will set you up to engage more intentionally with these questions on your own, and that it might even help you foster collaborative spaces where you can engage with these questions with others. I hope you see this book as a starting point, rather than a destination. My goal is to give you a rough basic structure to help contain reflections—and conversations—that can otherwise seem daunting in their vastness.

MOTIVATING INSIGHTS

This book is motivated and guided by four related insights.

The first is that we all live with ideas about ultimate questions, but often those ideas go unnoticed, unappreciated, and unmentioned. And when they become invisible, we miss opportunities to reflect on them, question them, consider alternatives to them, and through this process find better ways of thinking as well as living. For instance, we have ideas about religion and politics, but we "know" not to discuss those ideas in polite company. That reticence can lead us to sleepwalk through our lives. We might simply absorb notions about our purpose and identity that were handed down by parents or friends or role models. Or we might avoid thinking about these topics entirely. We might think, furthermore, that these questions are the exclusive playthings of philosophers, scientists, and various other extraordinary geniuses. We might feel like we have no right, or ability, to think about these questions on our own.

I think this kind of modesty is shortsighted. Philosophers take on these questions precisely because they matter to everyone, and the diversity of their views on them demonstrates that nobody can answer them for anyone else. Even if we don't talk about them or consciously consider them very often, we have ideas about our identity and purpose, the best path to happiness, and the right way to have relationships. These ideas operate deep within us, and in some sense we can't do without them. And yet we might feel like they are too private or personal to discuss or even think about, or that we're not really qualified to have them. And the practical effect of that feeling is that we don't examine these ideas. The challenge of the ultimate questions in this book is less to invent answers from the position of a blank slate, like an academic philosopher, and more to become aware of the ideas we already have. Only then can we decide if these deepest ideas and beliefs actually work for us. The four questions we focus on in this book are ones everyone already has ideas about, even if they've never sat down to consciously think about them.

Part of what makes these questions special is that they are unavoidable (even if you are sleepwalking through life, at some point you will have to confront them). They are baked into human existence, even though each individual decides how to answer them and how to live out those answers. All this is to say: This book isn't meant to push you in the direction of any particular answer, but to make you aware of the answers you already live with. This is also why I started this section with the famous quote from Socrates regarding the "unexamined life." He isn't asking us to become professional philosophers and read arcane texts; he is asking us to become aware of how we approach life and be willing to consider alternatives, especially when our current approach isn't serving us.

A second guiding insight is that this project is facilitated, rather than hindered, when we talk about ultimate questions with people who see things differently than we do. We are often scared to share our views and beliefs with others, particularly when those views and beliefs are core to who we are. Revealing our true beliefs and opening ourselves to questioning requires a real capacity for vulnerability and a willingness to have our views challenged: to see the world differently. And under the right conditions, those kinds of encounters can be revelatory—not just when they lead us to revise our beliefs, but also when they make us more vividly aware of those beliefs, and more willing to affirm them. Through this process, these ideas cease to be unexamined parts of our internal "operating system" that we weren't even aware of; they become conscious decisions about to approach life, however tentatively we might hold them.

Part of the challenge of doing this work is that from the day we are born until the day we die, larger forces shape how we approach life: our parents, our siblings, our friends, our community, and so on. As we grapple with the questions in this book, we live in a world made up of other people also grappling with these questions. And the answers we come up with separately influence each other. This isn't something to be lamented. Our ability as a species to adopt *shared fictions* has unlocked powerful forms of collaboration throughout our history. Our societies are governed by invented concepts like "money" and "nations" that shape how we live our lives. These shared fictions also make it possible for us to come up with ideas about identity, purpose, happiness, and coexistence, and to do so in ways that make sense to others. We want the answers to be powerful for other people. We don't want them to belong only to us. Our answers operate as signals that mark who we are. Shared fictions give us common rubrics that make communication and community—of which, of course, business is a part—possible.

At the same time, we don't want our answers to simply copy the shared fictions—or conform to the expectations—of our communities. In fact, as we struggle to define and live out our answers, our efforts often collide with the influence of others. We want the answers we come up with to be original, to be intimately our own, and we want to know that we chose them freely, even if they fit larger patterns that make them understandable to people who aren't us. Our answers are less powerful if they replicate what's already out there—like when you show up to a big social event and a peer is wearing exactly the same outfit. It's the special flair we add, the element of our own freedom to believe as we choose, that makes our answers so potent.

The third insight shaping this book emerges from this dilemma: Our answers to ultimate questions are both public and personal, private and shared. We live in community, and our answers are needed because they carve out a space for us in community, but they do so by marking the ways in which we're unique, individual, and free. Part of the challenge of thinking about ultimate questions is to identify our influences, so that we can be more intentional about how we use them. Our answers are never just given to us. At some level, we always have to author them ourselves. We can choose to author them in a way that copies prevailing models or in a way that departs from those models, but we can never entirely relinquish our freedom to choose. One important goal of this book is to give you tools to recognize your influences so that you can be more aware of your self-authoring and more equipped to pursue it with intention.

A final, related insight is that these questions tend to have a general dimension related to humans as a whole (the "we" form) and a personal dimension related to each of us as individuals (the "I" form). We need both dimensions because we don't come up with our ideas in isolation; they are informed by the shared fictions of our communities. The two forms of the question inform each other, and they reflect the ideas we carry around (sometimes unconsciously) about people in general as well as about the particular humans in front of us at any given time. The two dimensions—the "I" and the "we"—need each other; the "I" helps make sense of the "we" and vice versa. Susan isn't just Susan; she is also a human being, and much of what I need to know about her is based on the fact that she's a person like you and me in important ways. Yet if I just treat her as a nonspecific "human being" and don't incorporate what I know about her specifically—or try to learn more about her so I can have a richer picture of her—chances are she won't respond particularly well to me as a friend, acquaintance, colleague, or manager.

While this insight about the interplay of the "I" and "we" forms of ultimate questions is important for all the ways we relate to each other, it is especially important in a business context. Much of what stakeholder theory is about is updating our theory of humans ("Who are we?") as well as insisting that we need a theory of each individual person, since not everyone is the same. Far too often, managers allow the focus on greed (and the theory that financial incentives are what drive human behavior) to dominate their view of humans. That is why so many managers are willing to say to their employees, "Our people are our most important assets"—even though they don't really know what that means, let alone whether it is true. In many respects managers are worse off for saying it: Because it has zero credibility with most employees, it reinforces the idea that management doesn't care about them, doesn't understand them, and doesn't value them. As I've learned from my students, it actually makes people disengage from their work, the company, and its goals, as well as the leadership and people in the company. If they don't value or see me, why should I see or value them (or the company)?

If instead we acknowledge that people are motivated both by financial incentives and by being heard, seen, and valued as individuals, then managers can create different ways to gain employees' trust, commitment, and willingness to lead in the trenches (often without specific financial incentives for doing so). As a leader, I would need a better theory of people and workers in general to take this new approach, as well as an updated theory of individual workers (e.g., Who is Susan? What does she like to do? What interests her?) that is aligned with that larger theory yet customized by taking time to get to know the individuals. This is a version of the idea of mass customization—both general and particular at the same time.[7]

In business and in life, these are the everyday ideas I carry around in my head about how I see myself and others, what I expect of people and can get from them when we interact, and how we might interact differently to create experiences that we like better—ones that are more productive, more fun, more meaningful, more intimate, more customized. These ideas are in the background of everything we do and are why we are having the kind of life we have; we have just been trained not to see them, or to see them as settled and unchangeable. My hope is that this book will bring these background assumptions to the forefront of your mind, so that you can examine and evaluate them to enact the ones you think are best.

Thinking about ultimate questions is a lot like trying to build a home. The work can seem daunting if you feel like you have to design something that's completely unique and unprecedented, and if you have to build it entirely on your own. But that's not how the process has to work. In building a home, even one that has your special distinctive touch, you'd try to get some outside consultation and gather some of the existing knowledge on home construction. At the same time, you wouldn't postpone your house project until you have become an expert architect, builder, seismologist, geologist, engineer, electrician, and plumber, all in one. Most of us would find that exhausting, incredibly expensive, and time-consuming—not to mention diverting our attention and resources away from other things we'd like to do with our lives. At a certain point, you will have collected *enough* information and consultation to create a vision that has architectural integrity while still being uniquely yours. Similarly, it's up to you to decide how far to take these questions. You may decide to take certain "shortcuts" in some areas by relying on the knowledge and wisdom of others. And you may also decide to extensively gather information in other areas so that your answers are more fully informed by your own research. You may even feel like learning is its own reward. But ultimately, the goal can't be to achieve total knowledge (as that is impossible), nor to design a set of answers that's perfect (also impossible). I can only speak for myself, but I imagine that your goal may be similar to mine—to come up with answers I can live with, and live in.

We never fully arrive at our answers. They're always works in progress, even if we feel deeply attached to certain ideas and beliefs. To avoid getting lost in the vortex of deep thoughts, and to have time to do the other things you care about in life, you have to decide which questions and topics deserve the time and effort it takes to grapple with them—and which ones you can leave alone or save for another time. The point is to become more aware of how deeply ingrained these questions are in our own lives, to recognize the value of seeing them, and to reflect on how well our existing answers are working for us.

The good news is you may end up finding that your current answers are your right or "best" answers. This book is not about prioritizing change or encouraging you to reject what you believe. Indeed, it is meant to draw attention to the importance and inevitability of believing. It is about going from a place of not seeing or noticing what we believe (and therefore, possibly being unaware that our beliefs shape our actions) to one where we can see those beliefs. We can examine them, question them, consider alternatives, and then decide if they are our best options.

In this way, an unconscious process—where we may be captive to someone else's ideas that we aren't even aware of—becomes a conscious one. We gain clarity about what we believe and how we want that to shape our lives. In short, engaging with the ultimate questions helps us to be more confident that our operating system is truly ours and not just some invisible, background process that we never notice or question.

STRUCTURE OF THE BOOK

Before we turn to the questions themselves, let's preview what's to come in each chapter. My course is structured around four ultimate questions, and this book is built in the same way. Each chapter will tackle a specific ultimate question.

- Who are we, and who am I?
- Why are we here, and why am I here?
- What is the good life, and what is my good life?
- How should I get along with others?

I identified these four particular questions because they have to do with the deepest themes of human life: identity, purpose, the nature of human flourishing, and coexistence. I offer them in this order not because one causes the next—in some ways, they are difficult even to separate from each other—but because each opens out into the next, inviting more exploration. When we consider who we are, we open the question to why we are here; when we consider our purpose, we open up to how that is part of our good life; and when we consider our good life, we open up to how that affects others and how we can help others also work toward their good lives.

These questions occur when the innate human capacity for curiosity turns toward itself. As humans, we're saddled with a particular kind of consciousness: We encounter the world in a state of intelligent wonder.

When the questioning at the heart of our awareness turns to the being who is asking the questions, we must ask these questions of ourselves. Our wonder about the nature and function of things in the world leads us to wonder about our own identity and purpose. Our wonder about the feelings and experiences the world fills us with leads us to wonder about the kinds of feelings and experiences we want to have and the nature of a good life. And as we contemplate the first three questions, we're aware of people who answer the questions differently. We wonder how we should relate to these others and about the right way to coexist with them—including how our answers to the first three questions might impose costs or demands on others as well as what their answers might ask of us. If we think only of ourselves and what we want or need, we impair our ability to create a larger community of people where we can each "do our own thing" while also allowing others to do the same—a society that enables and encourages flourishing.

In the classroom, we draw on the reflections of some thinkers, researchers, and scientists to help shape the conversation. We use these scholars as starting points to see our own lives differently and to engage more intentionally with questions of identity, purpose, the good life, and relationships with others. Some readers might be hungry for a stronger point of view, a book that pushes boundaries or advances a novel intellectual approach; if you are, that's wonderful. I encourage you to explore the resources in appendix 2 and read those that most excite or challenge you. In this book though, I intentionally try not to come across as an authority or, worse, an external critic. In service to that goal, I hope you can reimagine these voices as simply jumping-off points, people like you and me who are struggling with the same issues and came up with their own individual answers—which you can then react to, respond to, reject, adapt, accept, or use to spark new ideas (or some combination of these), as you work toward finding your *own* answers.

Our thinking is all too easily shaped by outside influences—the great thinkers, sure, but also our parents, our teachers, our friends, our colleagues, our managers, and our religious and political organizations. My goal in the class isn't to doubt or reject these influences or the insights they provide for how to navigate life. Rather, it is to help students be more aware of them and to help them see more clearly the assumptions they live by every day, so that they are better able to ensure those views align with their best judgment. Taking on the challenge of this book may lead you back to the place you began—yet even if you find yourself there, your posture toward that wisdom and those answers to the ultimate questions will be more fully yours. Your understanding of other options and your engagement with people and ideas will help you see more fully the variety of ways to live in this world and the importance of choosing how you will engage with others. Doing this work is part of being human and is vital to your ability to connect with and know other people—which is part of allowing them to be more fully human as well. It is also about humility and recognizing that as bright, well educated, and insightful as we are, we can always learn from becoming more self-aware and from listening to others.

So, as I do in my class, I draw on a few insights from outside thinkers—not to produce a detailed or exhaustive account of everything that's been said on these subjects, nor to advocate any particular perspective, but simply to motivate your reflections on how you live your life. This book is not a philosophical encyclopedia or a source of answers. If you want to learn why Stoicism (or Buddhism, or Islam, or any other philosophy or religion) emerged as a vibrant philosophy, what its main tenets are, and how it might help you lead a different life, there are great resources out there. I draw on some ideas and wisdom from a variety of academic disciplines, but that variety is neither exhaustive nor representative. I am much more familiar with "Western" traditions, and the thinkers I have chosen reflect that bias. I invite you to be curious about other perspectives on these questions and to look for inspiration for your process of questioning beyond these pages. My main task here is to help you become more aware of these ultimate questions, to consider how they currently shape your life, and to come up with creative ways to continue to engage with them. I'm much more interested in helping my students and readers than I am in history or academic theories. The design and structure of this book are intended to reflect that approach.

And so, in each chapter, after remarks that I hope will help you survey some of the landscape of existing thought about these questions, I turn to the stories of individual students who have taken my course and wrestled with these questions in their own lives.

Alex Bleiberg and I interviewed more than twenty Darden graduates who had taken "Ultimate Questions" and asked them to talk about how the questions came up for them, how the conversations in class helped them see the questions differently, and how all of this has led them to new and different ways of seeing their lives and the choices in front of them. I've chosen five of those students and use their stories as touchstones. Reflections from the same five people appear in each chapter. I offer these quotes not because I think these people have come up with the "right" answers, but because their stories illustrate what it looks like to grapple with the questions, to see them emerge from a particular life story, and to decide how to navigate them on the path to a better life. A couple of notes about these interviews: First, out of respect for the privacy of our interviewees, I've disguised their names and identifying information, but their words are their own, and I'm grateful to them for sharing. And second, the interviews focus on their individual stories, so their answers emphasize the "I" versions of each question, rather than the "we."

After the "Student Voices" section, each chapter turns to you and how this work relates to your life. If you were my student, I would try to find a way to challenge you and get you to do the work that living with ultimate questions entails. Since that isn't possible, I instead offer some exercises, so that you can start to work through these questions for yourself. This section marks a pivot from me sharing ideas about ultimate questions to asking you to roll up your sleeves and start to engage with this work yourself. This may be challenging. You may feel primed and ready to go by the time you get to these sections, confident in your answers—and if so, that is great. The far more common experience (as I've seen with students) is that this work is humbling and can feel overwhelming. That is a completely normal and understandable response. After all, who am I (or who are you) to pretend to know the best (or right) answers to these questions? Living with ultimate questions shows that you get how big the questions are and how many ways there are to answer them. You may want to outsource your answers to a really smart friend, a wise elder, or an academic expert. Each of those people would have useful ideas to share. But the goal in this section is not to create an expert answer so much as to gain a deeper awareness of how you already answer this question, from your own lived experience, and then decide how you might improve, refine, or even reject that answer on the way to a "better" answer that serves you and those around you. It is more a matter of taking the time to reflect, listen to yourself, and maybe ask friends how they perceive your answers based on how you live your life—and then figure out where and how you can do better.

Once you have a solid start on an answer, consider whether your current answer is a good one or if it leaves something to be desired. In class, I often ask, "What would it take to change your mind?" This is partly so my students begin the process of opening their minds, but it's also meant to get them to start asking themselves what kinds of ideas or processes (e.g., the scientific method) might lead them to choose differently than they have before. And it's meant to help them see that whatever beliefs they have are, at some level, things they may come to see as mistaken, wrong (factually or morally), or not the best they can do. We can't fully engage with ultimate questions unless we remain open to such possibilities. We can't learn and grow if we aren't willing to challenge our own views as vigorously as we challenge the views of others (especially those who see the world differently than we do). We need to be ready to see that updating and revising our views, especially when we have good reasons for doing so, is a sign of strength—not of failure or weakness.

At the back of the book, I offer two appendixes with tools you can use throughout and after you're done reading these chapters. The first is "A Guide to Having Hard Conversations," a sort of meta-questioning exercise. The questions in this book get to the deepest assumptions and values we hold, and figuring out our answers is much better—more enjoyable and more fruitful—when we do it with other people. This guide should help you learn to approach those conversations in ways that foster vulnerability and safety. They are especially relevant for the material in chapter 4, where you will explicitly focus on how to get along with others. Conversations with people different from you and with whom you strongly disagree are some of the most challenging conversations you can have. If they don't go well, or if you don't bring the right approach, they can lead to meltdowns and hurtful arguments. They can even turn into physical confrontations. That is why it is so important to be intentional about such conversations, and this back-of-the-book guide offers some useful tools for approaching them as well as some exit ramps that can help you de-escalate a situation before it goes too far off track.

The second appendix is a set of resources and readings. These resources are just a start—they are meant not as authoritative answers, but simply as invitations to delve more deeply into these ideas in ways that might resonate with you and how you've answered the questions so far, to build on the momentum and the larger journey of living the ultimate questions. You are already living out your answers. It is better to be aware of them, understand how they are shaping the life you lead, and consider how you might approach them differently. You have more power than you think. Being more awake and aware allows you to become more of who you want to be—and to create richer experiences and relationships with others, especially once you get more comfortable talking about these questions and learning what truly matters to others.

WHY DO THIS WORK?

As the population rises and the interdependence among people increases, tensions between groups grow. We live in what feels like an increasingly anxious and fractured world—with seemingly insurmountable global challenges like poverty, inequality, racism, global warming, authoritarianism, and war, not to mention the unknowns of innovations like artificial intelligence.

Business is one of the most practical and daily ways we relate to each other. It is also both the source of and a potential solution to many of the problems we face on a global level. As we learn about ourselves and others by working through the ultimate questions in this book, we will also gain insight into what makes organizations "work" and how to leverage the ability of people to collaborate to create outstanding performance. As it turns out, every company has a set of answers to ultimate questions—even when those answers have very little to do with the stated mission on a plaque in the hallway. There is an implied (and understood) ethos in how people show up at a company and do their tasks each day: what the boss values and expects, how we should treat each other, and what it means to be a good employee. Are people just going through the motions and doing the bare minimum because they feel like what they do is unimportant or just to help some executives and shareholders earn a big payday? Or do they tap into something deeper for themselves and their fellow stakeholders—a sense that what they do matters, that their products truly help and serve customers, that their company values and improves the lives of employees, that the mission is lived out in how people show up and treat each other every day? There is a lot at stake in how companies frame what they do, especially for how people engage with their colleagues. This book will help you see that ultimate questions matter for organizations. Being able to see this dimension of what is going on all around us (even if we have previously been trained not to see it) not only helps us identify the hidden assumptions that have already been made—many of which should be seen as choices or even rejected—but it also reveals new ways of leading people, designing organizations, and creating outstanding performance that serves all key stakeholders.

Sometimes our encounters with ultimate questions are predictable: They reliably surface in rites of passage like high school graduation, a religious ceremony, or starting a job. But sometimes they come out of nowhere—a relationship suddenly begins or ends, we receive a devastating diagnosis, or we are unexpectedly laid off. These moments can cause us to see our lives in a whole new way. They can cause us to question the very foundations upon which we've built our lives. This book is an opportunity to think about these questions without the urgency of a major life event. I invite you to start now, not wait for those moments when you are forced to face these questions in a state of panic. I wrote this book to help you see that these questions exist—they are with us every day and all the time—and to give you tools to engage with them, to help you notice your answers and decide whether they survive scrutiny. Are they *your* answers? Do they help you live the life you want to live, or do they steer you toward a life chosen by others whose agendas you don't want or don't believe in?

We have many choices about how to show up each day and engage with life. Many of us spend our days (often unconsciously) trying to do anything but be present, aware, or authentic. A quick look around a classroom, a coffee shop, or a restaurant reveals how much we focus on engaging with technology rather than other people—and that we are more focused on dissecting the past or preparing for the future than on experiencing the present. In many respects we live life as time travelers in our own minds, going back and forth through our lives without even realizing that we are doing so. Being such a time traveler isn't a bad thing, yet doing it too often, without recognizing we are doing it and at the expense of taking time to be here now—that is a problem. Doing the work to be present and aware takes effort, energy, and expertise we often believe we lack. Our brains are wired to make us want to operate on autopilot and not use the resources required to engage with ultimate questions.

I promise you: You can engage with the questions. You can learn new things about yourself, the people you encounter, and the world around you. And the results of those efforts will make you want to continue to do this work long after you finish reading this book. As it turns out, this work can be fun! It can create incredible opportunities to get to know and connect with others, and it can open a whole new path for you. All it takes is the choice to do it and the courage to follow where the questions take you.

CHAPTER 1

WHO ARE WE, AND WHO AM I?

The nitrogen in our DNA, the calcium in our teeth, the iron in our blood, the carbon in our apple pies were made in the interiors of collapsing stars. We are made of starstuff.
—**CARL SAGAN**, *Cosmos*

There is no human nature, since there is no God to conceive it.
—**JEAN-PAUL SARTRE**, *Existentialism and Human Emotions*

So God created man in his own image, in the image of God he created him; male and female he created them.
—Genesis 1:27

Keep looking at the bandaged place.
That's where the light enters you.
—**JALAL AL-DIN RUMI**, translated by Coleman Barks

Ultimate questions arise when we start to wonder—to reflect not just on the outside world and why things are as they are, but also on ourselves. They happen because of the weird way humans live in the world. We're saddled with a peculiar kind of consciousness. Other kinds of creatures have consciousness too, but their consciousness (as far as we can tell) tends to take things as they are. When a bee pollinates a flower, it understands the flower as a place to get nectar. As far as we know, it doesn't think about the flower any more than that. A beaver chews through a tree to build its dam; it knows what to do with the tree, but as far as we know, it doesn't stop to consider why the tree is that way.

Humans are different (though, as we learn more about them, these differences get smaller and harder to discern). We also make use of flowers and trees. But when we interact with them, our thoughts don't stop at how we use them, or even at new ways we might use them. We also tend to ask about their nature, their relationship to other things, where they come from, and what makes them unique. And we do this often without consciously choosing to—it seems to be part of being human. Our awareness doesn't give us these answers; instead, it confronts us with the questions. And it is these questions that make human consciousness unique. They're not just what our awareness does; they are also what it *is*. Awareness isn't a closing but an opening, not an answer but a question. Awareness isn't a state of knowing but a state of wondering, an inclination to fill in the blanks where our bare senses leave gaps. It's an empty space where conjecture, theory, story, and speculation can come rushing in. It's the absence of an answer as well as the ongoing effort to fill that absence.

And that brings us to ask ultimate questions. If awareness is a question or set of questions, *ultimate* questions are what happen when awareness looks in the mirror. When we look at things in the world, we can't help but wonder what they are. Inevitably, though, we wonder about what, or who, is doing the wondering. We ask ourselves, "Who am I?" This question takes place at the root of human awareness. It happens when human awareness turns in on itself. We are here, we are alive, and there are many things about being alive that are great. We enjoy a good meal, a hug from a loved one, watching a sunrise or sunset, telling a funny story, spending time with friends. There are lots of things we do and enjoy doing. But what do all these facets of our existence tell us about who we are as beings? Do we have an essential nature that exists for all of us, despite the vast number of ways in which each person seems different and unique? What is this "humanity" we all share? And how am I, even as a human being, different from other humans?

As we think about ourselves, we imagine ourselves as individuals, but we also imagine the larger category of beings that we belong to. The two sides of the question feed into each other. I am the kind of creature that I am because I'm a human being. And humanity as a whole is made up of all the individual creatures that are human, in our own unique and different ways.

WHO ARE WE?

So let us start with the more general form of the question and see how it leads us to consider the more specific one. Who are we? René Descartes famously founded his philosophy on the principle that a person's existence can be proven by the fact that they think and doubt (here's that awareness again): "I think, therefore I am." Some maintain that as humans, we were put on the earth by God, who created this planet for us and "created humans in his image . . . and said to them, 'Be fruitful and multiply and fill the earth and subdue it and have dominion over . . . every living thing.'"[1] Others see humans not as lords of our domain, but as beings in community with other living creatures in a vast web of interdependence.[2]

One of my favorite parts of teaching the "Ultimate Questions" course is having the class tackle this first half of the first ultimate question ("Who are we?") in a very preliminary way, on the second day of class. I give the students a variety of different readings and then have them form groups to come up with their own definitions of who we are, in four sentences. It is an impossible task, yet it always helps me better understand my students. I am amazed at how they're able to reflect on their entire life experience with other humans, as well as their own identity, and then come up with a short paragraph that somehow captures their sense of what is most important about being human.

What is equally fascinating is how much the students' answers are influenced by the readings I assigned—most recently, these included sections from Joshua Greene's *Moral Tribes*, Yuval Noah Harari's *Sapiens*, and David Brooks's *The Road to Character*. Based on these, even though I took great pains to frame these readings as spurs to conversation rather than sources of unquestionable truth, students tended to focus on an evolutionary view and on the search for a shared morality. I could have just as easily assigned, say, Hannah Arendt's *The Origins of Totalitarianism*, Sun Tzu's *The Art of War*, and Alan Turing's "Computing Machinery and Intelligence."[3] This tendency in how my students respond reinforces to me the human tendency to imitate, try to do what pleases, and let our thinking be shaped by what is most recent and familiar.

So let's step into my students' shoes. How might you answer the question?

To kick-start the process of thinking about human nature, let's examine a few ways it's been tackled in myth, philosophy, and social science. Many of our traditions provide a kind of self-portrait, a codebook for how we have perceived ourselves throughout the ages. Folklore and fairy tales paint a messy and complicated picture. They act as storehouses of the ideas we've had about ourselves, because they show us contending with the forces of magic and nature, with demons, spirits, animals, and gods. They reveal beliefs about our place in the chain of being and illustrate how the people who told those stories viewed our role in the larger cosmos. The characters in them show humanity at its kindest and its most cruel, most trustworthy and most cunning, most generous and most selfish, most capricious and most deliberate. People are at the mercy of larger forces but nonetheless have inklings of power and mastery, a capacity to play the trickster and outmaneuver these larger forces (think of the many stories of humans outwitting giants: Odysseus and the cyclops, David and Goliath, Jack and the beanstalk). Historically, it's been these stories that have told us who we are, whether we're fooling giants or receiving the gift of fire. What they show is a creature that possesses the ability to change and adapt, but within limits. If we follow Joseph Campbell, we might see patterns in these stories across place, time, culture, language, religion, and traditions: There is a "hero with a thousand faces" who lives within all these stories.[4] That is, Campbell makes the case that there is a common thread of understanding of a "hero": the path they must follow, the heroic act(s) they must do, and how their heroism shapes both the hero and their community. Even though the details can vary dramatically, there are important commonalities to notice across this practice to illustrate the (partial) unity of human consciousness.

We can be kind and generous to our fellow creatures in one moment and capable of unthinkable cruelty in the next. We are curious, playful, and energetic. We are willing to sacrifice (to the point of giving up our lives) for strangers, but we've also shown an ability (even a tendency) to build concentration camps, to commit genocide, to enslave and dominate others whom we define as "less than."

Social scientists have a range of views about what makes humans unique. We're often competitive with each other. Our history is full of examples of this impulse, of the passionate struggle for wealth, power, and domination. The specter of competition has raised armies, spurred the growth of technology, and inspired civilizations. We might be occasionally self-motivated apart from competition, but get us in a room with rivals and see how certain of those motivations are amplified while others recede. Many economists celebrate the competitive aspect of human nature, portraying humans as *Homo economicus* driven by a quest for endless accumulation, aiming always to seek personal, individual benefit and consistently making rational, objective choices to do so.[5] Others, like Nobel laureate Elinor Ostrom, complicate this view, arguing that collective goals and actions are motivators that are just as strong.[6]

Evolutionary biologists and psychologists, too, have called attention to both the competitive and communal aspects of our nature. Early evolutionary theory focused, of course, on competition—Charles Darwin's concept of survival of the fittest has been used to justify cruelty and enshrine inequality—but, as with economics, evolutionary theorists have added nuance. For example, primatologist and ethologist Frans B. M. de Waal found strong evidence of altruism and cooperation in humans and our close evolutionary cousins, chimpanzees.[7] Evolutionary anthropologist Michael Tomasello argues for the uniquely human aspects of cooperation—what he calls *shared intentionality*, or the ability to imagine what another person is thinking and work with them toward a common goal, irrespective of individual gains.[8] But even among those theorists focusing on cooperation, the picture they've painted isn't entirely rosy. As these researchers highlight the collaborative elements of our humanity, they find that our ability to cooperate can create new types of rivalry and conflict. For example, one empirical study found that people trusted each other more if they were more similar to each other, ethnically, socially, and economically,[9] and that higher levels of trust were linked with more investment,[10] further benefiting the in-group. There is considerable evidence that humans, like higher primates, form communities of affiliation that view outsiders distrustfully. The groups we create also tend to be organized into hierarchies, with leaders wielding power over the rest of the members.

And evolutionary biologists are perhaps more pessimistic than economists about the human capacity for reason. Neoclassical economists celebrate human rationalism, touting our supposedly innate capacity to pursue enlightened self-interest (though, again, these claims have been troubled by empirical evidence). Scholars from such diverse fields as evolutionary biology, cognitive psychology, history, and political science highlight how our in-group bias can undermine our objectivity and weaken our ability to think logically.[11] They show how we filter information through the lens of our group, making stories far more powerful than facts in shaping how we see the world and determining who and what we trust.

So these are two modern angles on the question "Who are we?": first, neoclassical economics—in which humans are inherently selfish, individualistic, and competitive, rationally pursuing our interests in a way that spontaneously creates rough systems of coordination powered by greed—contrasted with economic theories that highlight cooperation; and second, two general strands in evolutionary biology that define humans by competition or by cooperation, collaboration, and even altruism (which can then lead to intergroup competition). Both domains focus on how we relate to each other, where on the continuum between competition and collaboration we are at any given moment. Rather than an either/or (i.e., we are either competitive or cooperative), human behavior appears to be malleable and shaped by a variety of individual and contextual factors. So, for some purposes we can come up with a quick catchphrase to capture the essence of being human, but to have a fuller picture, we might need several catchphrases to bring in more of the nuance—and maybe even a book if we want our curiosity to be thoroughly satisfied. We just rarely have time to write (or read) that book, especially when we are in the middle of an activity like kicking a soccer ball with friends. We need an implicit theory to help us understand what is going on, why people do what they do, and why each of us responds the way we do.

There are, of course, many other perspectives we could use to glean an answer to the question. We could certainly drill down further into economics and evolutionary theory. And we could consider harder sciences as well: From a chemical perspective, we are nothing more than bags of water. Our physical bodies carry us like walking puddles, keeping the water in our tissues protected and replenished. To adopt a more biological view, we're the carriers of a particular human code in our DNA, one that furnishes us with highly sophisticated organs of adaptation: thumbs that can grasp, a musculoskeletal system that allows us to stand upright, a respiratory apparatus that allows us to speak. From the perspective of neuroscience, we are defined by our brains: Their immense complexity compared to the brains of other creatures allows us to perform much higher forms of mental activity, to compute and create and imagine rather than to simply regulate and react. Some of us define human nature entirely on the basis of our intellect, focusing on our capacity to think, to have awareness, and to control our impulses. Yet others highlight our capacity for love, which transcends simple blood relations or any kind of logic. We write poetry and dance. We celebrate our creativity and experience joy in life. Our human nature reveals itself in so many ways that resist simple and sweeping claims about who we are as beings.

These perspectives, whether based on double-blind experiments or intuitions of beauty, are all stories, shared fictions of one kind or another—which points to one important aspect of our collaborative nature that can be so second nature that it gets overlooked: language. Language is one of the most fundamental things about us.[12] But precisely because it's so fundamental, it can seem less important than the flashier aspects of our existence, such as our penchant for fighting wars, courting a life partner, or traveling to outer space. In fact, though, we live in language: Our very understanding of reality takes place through and in words (objects whose meanings are, by definition, understood by other humans). And alongside our linguistic capacity is the ability, and the primal need, to share stories. Throughout history we've needed to tell stories about ourselves and our lives, to let others know who we are and what we do. It might be easier to pay attention to the glossier aspects of our history, episodes of conquest and domination, but we know about these episodes today only because of the quieter but constant hum of our storytelling traditions. Across multiple early groups of humans, researchers have found evidence of cave drawings—people taking time to create images of things happening in their lives for others to see. While we might find this ordinary, anthropologists take this as a powerful indication of the kind of beings we are, especially since this was happening in so many places at the same time.[13] We are tool-using, technological beings, and we are also art-making, creative beings—we modify our environment to represent one or more realities.

Indeed, today, in the 2020s, we might be tempted to answer the question of who we are by highlighting our relationship to a very specific kind of technology. We seem particularly dependent on computer-based and internet technology, and some of us even want to merge with it, to make it part of our bodies and how our minds work. It seems like we're constantly engaged with our digital devices, even in the midst of the so-called quality time we spend with friends and loved ones. Today you might find a romantic couple "enjoying" a delicious meal at a high-end restaurant by scanning their phones and texting their friends. Young children have an amazing facility with smartphones and similar devices and can operate them far more intuitively than their parents and grandparents can. What do these behaviors tell us about who we are and where we're going as a species? Is our nature determined by the tools we develop? Do the capabilities that allow us to shape our world so powerfully also define who we are? Is *Homo sapiens* really *Homo technologicus*? Taking it further, some predict that we will manipulate both computing and genetic technology to become cybernetic beings that are an even greater version of ourselves. Faced with such powerful tools and a desire to serve future generations, are we destined to make these choices, or will we resist the temptation and chart a different course? Rather than the end of evolution, is *Homo sapiens* just a point of transition to another kind of being that will move beyond us—just like we did with the Neanderthals? If we are the children of God, ought we not to incorporate these powers into who we are so we can fulfill our destiny and better rule over this planet, and perhaps the galaxy? Or should we instead follow the Buddhist principle that "an action is good if it leads to freedom from suffering" and focus our use of artificial intelligence on decreasing pain and suffering?[14]

The near-constant stream of news about AI and social media and other ways we relate to our technology is a communal story, an ongoing discussion in the 2020s. And communal stories or shared fictions are what make human cooperation, on a large scale, possible. Such stories can take the form of founding narratives, giving unrelated groups of people a shared identity as part of a tribe or nation. But they can also take more mundane forms, furnishing us with the concepts that keep society humming. Absent these communal fictions, it's very hard for people to really know each other well enough to work effectively as a group. Under "ordinary" conditions, social scientists have capped the number of strangers who can work together successfully at 150 people.[15] What made that number grow, and what allowed for more widespread forms of cooperation, was the invention of these shared fictions.[16] Some commonplace shared fictions are "money," "nations," and "corporations." Such ideas are wholly fabrications. They do not exist except in our minds. But they've become so ingrained in human existence that we have trouble imagining the world without them. If I have a US-government-issued dollar bill with a picture of George Washington on it, I know without anyone telling me that its worth is "one dollar." On its own, it's nothing more than a piece of paper covered with ink. But in the context of our shared fictions, it has a meaning. Money works only because we all (or at least the vast majority of us) believe it is real.

Such fictions are hugely important because they allow kinds of collaboration among humans that are far more elaborate and complex than would otherwise be possible. *Homo sapiens* wasn't able to dominate the Neanderthals because of any physical advantage: In many respects, the Neanderthals were physically superior and would have likely prevailed in a one-to-one competition. In groups, however, modern humans were far more effective, largely because of their ability to form plans together and to forge the shared intentionality necessary to operate as a team. This team coordination, which allowed groups of humans to adapt in real time, was what made them such potent adversaries. As Yuval Noah Harari explains, "Neanderthals could share information about the whereabouts of lions, but they probably could not tell—and revise—stories about tribal spirits. Without an ability to compose fiction, Neanderthals were unable to cooperate effectively in large numbers, nor could they adapt their social behaviour to rapidly changing challenges."[17]

I highlight all these perspectives not in order to bewilder you with options, but to illustrate something about our human essence. It's easy to get lost in the maze when we try to fix an answer to the question "Who are we?" Humans can legitimately be, at various times, cooperative and competitive, violent and friendly, loving and hateful, observant scientists and fantastical painters, highly rational and deeply religious. We might say that it's context that brings out whichever aspect of our human nature we happen to see at any given moment. But it might be more accurate to say that human nature is intrinsically unfixed. Recall our discussion of fairy tales: Their answer to the question "Who are we?" is a kind of nonanswer. The human heroes of these stories are "defined" by their ability to change shape, to wear disguises, and to invent tricks in order to contend with much more powerful beings. Their humanity is an inner germ of self-invention.

Our very ability to pose the question, to ask ourselves who we are, suggests that we're able to do something about it, to act differently because we know this about ourselves. Perhaps that's what makes us unique in the first place: that we're able to imagine ourselves as having a nature, which then enables us to mold that nature. In this view, "Who are we?" is a question that is answered not by who we are but by what we do and what we can imagine. It's not something we discover so much as something we invent. It's a kind of story we tell about ourselves, one that relies on facts and experience and history—but also our values and goals. And reflecting on that story as we write it enables us to understand ourselves and each other better.

WHO AM I?

Telling that story about who we are is important in its own right, but it also starts us thinking about the more personal aspect of the question. And if it's important to have some sense of who we are in order to know the world we live in, it's just as important to think about the question of "Who am I?" to know the person trying to live, work, and play in that world.

Shifting to the "I" form of the question moves us away from the general traits and tendencies of humans and more toward the quirks, distinctive aspects of our personality, and unique bits of our own history that make our lives *ours*. And if we truly want to know another human person, we also want to know what makes them *them*: their history, hobbies, aspirations, sense of humor, favorite smell or brand of perfume. Taking this turn leads us to downplay the textbooks on human biology, psychology, linguistics, and sociology that give us a picture of the "we" and to focus more fully on the realm of stories, individual human experiences, and identity, to find what makes each of us unique among humans.

As we think about how to answer "Who am I?," we can consider some of the strategies people tend to use when they move from considering humanity as a whole to considering individual humans. Humans can be grouped in so many ways: by language, culture, gender, heritage, geographical location, religion, personality type, age—the list goes on—and these features do matter in our understanding of ourselves and each other. There are whole industries that use science (or pseudoscience) to answer the question of "Who am I?" in the larger context of the question "Who are we?" Some of these industries come out of psychology and the study of personality: The Big Five personality test assigns each person a score on five personality "dimensions"; Myers-Briggs divides people into types based on four traits.[18] Other industries attempt to answer the question using our genetics: Companies like Ancestry use DNA markers to comb our ancestry and ethnic makeup, and maybe one day genetic tests will tell us in more detail about our inborn habits and dispositions.[19] Alongside these "scientific" approaches are more mystical traditions like astrology, which were once regarded as scientific (even if they aren't anymore).

These approaches might come from a variety of disciplines and enjoy a greater or lesser level of credibility. But they have one thing in common:

They all tackle identity through classification. They work by assigning each of us a category, based on certain fixed traits that make us who we are. Even genetic science, which has already resulted in a complete map of the human genome, can tell us what makes us genetically unique only through comparison and categorization of versions of traits.[20]

You might feel like the information provided by these kinds of methods tells us all we need to know about ourselves. And these assessments are widespread for a reason—they give us data that helps us grapple with who each of us is. According to *The New York Times*, personality testing is a $2 billion industry.[21] You may feel like your Myers-Briggs type or your placement on the Enneagram scale tells you all you need to know about yourself.[22] But for many of us, the answers provided by these tests feel incomplete and unsatisfying.

After all, tests like Myers-Briggs and the Enneagram assign us to types. That means, by definition, that they don't capture what makes each of us, as a particular individual, unique. Even the rare types of Myers-Briggs personalities show up in millions of people. What these tests are trying to do is to assign our individual identity to a category, an archetype, and to fill out what that archetype looks like in general. The very premise of tests like Myers-Briggs and the Big Five is that people can be divided into what we might call personality herds, nonethnic classifications that have appeared throughout human history to make up its complex tapestry. These tests identify some things that are distinct about who each of us is, yet they lump us in with a huge number of other humans—millions, and possibly billions, of other humans have these same traits. They don't get to all the complexity and uniqueness that make me uniquely me—and they don't mean that my desire to craft an individual life that is mine (and not just the life of my Myers-Briggs type) is for naught.

If you're unsatisfied with these kinds of "scientific" approaches and their labels, you might try to answer the question "Who am I?" in a way that rejects labels. You might craft an identity that acknowledges your feeling of yourself as infinitely unique. After all, no one lives in your own mind except you. Maybe your identity is made up of the many strange and unique things that go on in your mind. Maybe you can answer the question by paying close attention to what goes on there. We might call this approach Jamesian, in honor of the philosopher William James, who famously described the sensory experience of babies: "The baby, assailed by eyes, ears, nose, skin, and entrails at once, feels it all as one great blooming, buzzing confusion."[23] James also coined the term *stream of consciousness*: "Consciousness . . . does not appear to itself chopped up in bits. Such words as 'chain' or 'train' do not describe it fitly as it presents itself in the first instance. It is nothing jointed; it flows."[24] When we turn toward ourselves and answer the question "Who am I?," perhaps we should embrace James's blooming, buzzing confusion. What is our identity, after all, other than our uniqueness? And what is our uniqueness other than our stream of consciousness, the strange, often unbidden thoughts and ideas that come into our mind? No one before or after you in history will ever have the exact same thoughts and ideas you've had.

Still, even keeping a careful list of all the thoughts we've ever had, as arduous and long-winded a task as that might be, would only give us part of the picture. When we think about our *identity*, we're thinking about something that can be communicated to someone else, that has a meaning. The verbalization of all the strange thoughts and feelings we've ever had doesn't add up to a meaning on its own, precisely because it lacks the labels and concepts that would give it sense, interpretation, and order. Not every thought or experience is the same, even for us in our own minds; some things matter more, cut closer to who we are and how we see the world.

To figure out what kind of answers might work when we ask about our own identity, it helps to think about what answers work when we ask about the identity and nature of other things.

How do we grapple with the identity of (for example) natural objects? Most of us can pretty easily identify a tree. At the same time, most of us have a very hard time describing that identity. Defining a tree is much harder than looking out the window and pointing out the trees one sees there. The reason it's easy to identify a tree, and yet difficult to define a tree's identity, has to do with the kind of answers we give when we're wondering about a tree's nature. Those answers encompass a lot. When we think about the nature of trees, we're aware of what they look like, how tall they sometimes are, their genetic and evolutionary relation to other plants, the relation of plants as a whole to other living beings. We think about their history, their uses, their beauty, the cycle of their seasonal rebirth. We even think about their spiritual power, the metaphors they're used in, the roles they play in our own and other cultures' mythologies, and their interrelatedness to and dependence on all the other beings in their ecosystem. Our idea of the nature of a tree is never just one thing. It's open. It's flexible depending on what we are thinking about, what mood we are in, and what purpose we are trying to serve (e.g., are we wondering at the tree's beauty and the spiritual power it has, or considering how to harness its strength to build our new cabin?). Our idea of a tree can grow (figuratively and literally). It can take in new angles, new episodes, new perspectives, without collapsing. It is built on a whole branching root system of associations. But it's also not awash in blooming, buzzing confusion because it doesn't depend on every detail that could be known about every tree. The idea doesn't need *all* those details to have a meaning.

Our idea of the "nature" of a tree is a kind of story. It can take in many strands and threads, and it can drop or add new threads over time, but it takes all those threads together and weaves them into something that allows us to say, when we're in the woods somewhere, that that over there is a tree. To point to a tree in the woods, we don't have to know all the threads that went into that story, and in fact we never *can* know all the threads. And yet together they add up to something that we're aware of as a single idea and that makes identifying a tree possible. They add up to meaning.

Our answers to the question "Who am I?" thread the same needle between science and confusion, a desire for structure and certainty and a sense of wonder and mystery. The answers have to be not only meaningful, but also open and dynamic. And so one way to answer the question "Who am I?" is to develop something between a fixed label and an ever-changing stream—something like a story. Stories are vehicles that endow each of us with uniqueness, while still holding us to a common order that makes sense. They combine description and a sense of history with aspiration, discovery with invention.

STUDENT VOICES

Now that we have some perspectives from myth, science, and philosophy, we'll turn to the perspectives of several of my students on this question of "Who am I?" They, like all of us, are grappling with these questions—this work is never finished. Even when our views seem fairly fixed and settled, they evolve as we grow and change and have new experiences. This section provides a chance to see how these questions come up for five of my former students—what experiences these questions bring to mind, what parts of their stories they're wrestling with, how their current answers are either serving them or holding them back. Their comments about ultimate questions are one way (or, in this case, five ways) to reflect on these questions, to see where the questions show up, where they find them to be difficult to understand or navigate, and how the questions interact with their hopes and dreams. Their words can provide clues for you about what to pay attention to, how to make sense of these questions in your life, how to use the process of questioning to form new meanings and possibilities. Think of this section less as a way to get "good" or "right" answers and more as a window into understanding how others like you do this work.

ROBERT

When he considers who he is, Robert marvels at how external events changed him in ways he couldn't have expected. From a young age, he wanted to be an elected official, but his path began to diverge from his plans when he was caught stealing at just thirteen years old. When he appeared before a judge—a crisis bound to bring on thoughts of ultimate questions—he admitted that wanting to fit in had led him to make bad choices. He asks himself, "What if I hadn't been arrested when I was thirteen? Maybe I would have kept succumbing to peer pressure. Instead, I had to break up with my seventh-grade girlfriend, was grounded the entire summer, and then spent two years reading poetry and being an introvert and reading a lot of books." He points to this summer and his reading as leading to his decision to start a program teaching chess to incarcerated people so they could learn strategic thinking. And in turn, as a result of that teaching experience, Robert learned he liked teaching and volunteered for Teach for America after graduation. He was teaching at an elementary school in New Jersey on September 11, 2001, and in response to the attack on the World Trade Center that day, he decided to join the Army National Guard and did a tour in Iraq, where he was involved in an accident that impaired his ability to have children. After his tour, he attended law school, then worked for the government. After his older brother, whom he'd idolized and envied, died from a drug overdose, he took a job at a pharmaceutical company. In his first week there, the CEO advised him to pursue an MBA, which led him to Darden and my "Ultimate Questions" course.

As he tells it, "I wonder if perhaps all of life's forces are reactionary forces. Or is that just my mirror image reflection from my experiences? But that's been something that I've thought about before. Tying that back into my accident, what does it all mean? What if I wasn't supposed to have a kid? I don't join the army but for 9/11. I don't teach inner-city school but for the fact that I like teaching people in prison and I felt good about making a difference. I don't teach people in prison but for the fact that I read this book [about how chess develops strategic thinking]. I don't join a pharma company probably but for the fact that my brother overdosed on drugs." One way to read this story is that he consistently learns from disaster and finds ways to respond in ways that help the larger community: He gets caught stealing, so he helps prisoners; he is nearby when the Twin Towers are attacked, so he defends his country; his brother dies of an overdose, so he works on nonopioid pharmaceuticals. But Robert writes his story in a different way, with several competing throughlines. He acknowledges his impulse to "give back" while at the same time describing his interest in teaching chess as mostly decided by his longtime fascination with strategy and manipulation. He characterizes himself as curious and passionate about making a difference, while at the same time arguing that ambition is a stronger force for him. And instead of seeing his reactions to events as constructive, intentional responses, he considers himself a passive recipient of the twin forces of "some sort of spiritual help . . . that's beyond my comprehension [that is] guiding us or helping us" and, in what seems like a contradiction, pure physics and chance, which he characterizes as "a Ping-Pong ball bouncing around into who we ultimately become."

JOSHUA

Unlike Robert, Joshua does see himself as an active force in his own life and the lives of others, and he sees a consistent line from his early experiences through to his adulthood.

After he graduated from Darden, Joshua pursued a career in IT. As a Black man in a field dominated by white men, he had a bit of an identity crisis. "Being a Black guy in IT, I definitely did not feel like I had a place at the table. I did not feel like I could have a voice, and I also felt like I was minimized. . . . [I asked myself], 'Is this an area, a career that I could excel in? Can I see myself being in an organization that does not have any executive leadership that looks like me? How much do I, or must I, conform and change my identity—who I am, who I have always been—to either placate, to look like, to resemble, to assimilate to those [in the field]?' . . . It's been a huge struggle."

The struggle was familiar, though, to Joshua, which may have helped him navigate it. He was raised by his grandfather, a military veteran, pastor, and leader in local government and nonprofit organizations. His grandfather saw himself as a "button pusher," by which he meant someone who would push against the status quo. He bought a house in an all-white neighborhood in a midsize city in the southern United States, and he always spoke his mind. Joshua grew up in the only Black family in an all-white neighborhood; some of his neighbors flew Confederate flags. At the same time, he felt like an outsider in his Black church because he didn't live in the same neighborhoods as the other congregants. He remembers basketball as a "great equalizer": "We would play basketball together. And [that] allowed me to home in on being a part of, or welcomed . . . within the communities, the Black community specifically, even though I didn't live in the Black community." Basketball also helped him connect with non-Black friends: "A lot of my friends that I was able to make that were not Black probably came from basketball. And we still stay in contact. . . . Where there are common themes that we all have, where you break those barriers, you break what may be those external forces, . . . there is some commonality that we can connect to."

So as a child, Joshua felt out of place both at home and in church but found a sense of belonging on the basketball court. He definitely did not feel this in his first two jobs out of college. As he tells it, "In my first two jobs, I was trying to come up to speed so I could feel like I could have a voice, and I would not speak up at all. I would not speak up when it came to technical things, because I didn't feel like I was confident or comfortable adding any type of dialogue around where the group or team was trying to head."

As he gained confidence in his abilities, though, he realized how important it was for him to use his voice in professional settings, and to communicate an authentic representation of himself—maybe not in spite of but because he hadn't at first felt like he belonged. He now answers the question of "Who am I?" partly by emphasizing the power of his own voice: "I'm not going to be silenced. I'm also going to let you know how I feel . . . I'm going to let you hear and give you my thoughts. You're going to hear my voice and my feedback as well."

Joshua's understanding of himself has, as it does for all of us, several dimensions: He is a Black man in IT, the grandson of a Black pastor who grew up in a white neighborhood, a basketball player, and a business-school graduate—to say nothing of the many other roles he plays in his personal and professional life. His experience in the "Ultimate Questions" class, and then in conversation with Alex and me after he'd graduated, helped him clarify one primary aspect of that selfhood: a person who breaks barriers, pushes buttons, and challenges the status quo, not only (as one might expect based on his story and our shared fictions) through his own efforts to excel as a member of an underrepresented demographic, but much more so through his efforts to include everyone, to listen to every voice, especially as a manager: "It's all about knowing how I show up, and I'm going to give anybody that time and attention and care as long as that is what they want from me. And even if they don't, I'm always available."

Joshua defines himself in response to external perceptions: He breaks barriers set up by racist assumptions. Liniksha's experience puts those perceptions in even sharper relief.

LINIKSHA

Having grown up in Southeast Asia and immigrated to the United States when she was eighteen, Liniksha was surprised at how people's ideas about her changed with her move. She grew up with institutionalized misogyny: She calls her home country "a society that is so hard on women . . . especially single women . . . [who do] not even get property rights or rights to inheritance." In the United States, she confronted racism instead. She recalls, "I wasn't aware of my race until I came to the United States. I would just see myself as a person, but people would see me as a Brown woman. And no matter what I did, that wouldn't go away. . . . So, in a sense, I gave up a lot of sexism, and I took some racism. And this is still the life that I choose to live, because the concentration of sexism in my [home] environment was not . . . working for me. I'm better equipped to handle this." Although she did deal with such things as her college boyfriend's family rejecting her because she was not white, her release from sexism was freeing: "Being confident, being stubborn, being too much—I was always too much [in my home country]—in the United States, that was no longer the case. I wasn't stubborn, I was driven. I wasn't arrogant, I was confident. . . . I didn't change. But the way the world perceived me changed dramatically . . . and it filled me with so much confidence. I used to have a hard time getting the right grades, or just being my best, because I didn't realize how much the external circumstances brought me down. The moment external circumstances became positive, it was just so easy to succeed—academically, personally, professionally." She graduated from college with a 4.0 grade point average, enrolled at Darden, and worked at a succession of prestigious jobs.

External perceptions matter. They have real effects. Liniksha's move to the United States led to a new understanding of herself, and without the sexism she'd internalized and let bring her down, she was able to find confidence and excellence. As she considered this first ultimate question, "Who am I?," she was more aware of both how others perceived her and how she perceived herself, internally.

This experience of wrenching away long-held assumptions also brought on reflection "on the spiritual level, on an atomic level," she describes. "I grew up in an abusive household," she discloses. "I'm a survivor of child abuse, which is why I wanted to come to the United States and build my way here by academic excellence. That was my safety." With her US move, she cut ties with her mother. This second, more internal freedom is now a defining factor in her self-perception: "I want my survivorship to mean something. Less than 1 percent of people who went through what I went through survive, let alone be here [in the United States, with an MBA]. So I want my existence to mean something. Something for myself and those around me. . . . Corporate America is not meant for people like me. It was designed for the able-bodied male archetype. But I'm not married to corporate America. [My identity] is not a clean-cut thing, you know, like 'Oh, this happened. And now here's where I am, and here's what I'm going to do.' But now I'm listening to my voice above everyone else's. Above [my mother's] primarily. I guess that, to me, is how you know that you are being captured by somebody, and you're a hostage to somebody, is when you listen to their voice in your head above your own. And so, I finally feel free. I felt free when I came to America for the time, physically. But internally I finally feel free for the first time."

ADANNA

Adanna also struggles with a mismatch between her self-perception and external perceptions of her. But though she is also a nonwhite immigrant—she grew up in an African country, went to boarding school in Europe, and is now a US citizen—the mismatch she takes issue with is unrelated to her race or gender. In answering the "Who am I?" question, she highlights her desire to be known for her intelligence rather than her personality: "Something that I struggle with is that I tend to get a lot of positive feedback about my personality. I tend to get 'Oh, you're a really nice person. It is great to work with you.' At work, and I think it has to do with my academic upbringing, I always separate those things, like 'Yes, I have a great personality! But that's me being me, and it's almost effortless.' What I want to be known for is my academic side. Did I build that financial model well? Or did I present this well? But I guess impact is impact, . . . whether it's from my personality or my brain. I think I tend to take the personality side of things for granted, because it doesn't feel like effort, so I don't value the reward. And therefore, when I do things that I put a lot of effort into, I care a lot more about the reward. I'm trying to just embrace that I'm a package, and therefore there's no point trying to divvy up what that impact looks like."

She places value on the things she has to work hardest for, perhaps a relic of her many international moves or her rigorous boarding schools. But as part of her process through the ultimate questions, she's realizing that while she values hard work, she can at the same time pick and choose where to focus her efforts. When she found applying to business school easy, she devalued it and nearly missed out on enrollment. She reflects now on that experience: "I'm trying to just accept the fact that there are a lot of different aspects of life that are hard. And there's so many other places, especially as a Black woman in the world, where I would need to fight for my place. So, the few times where it's actually easy, I need to accept that and conserve my energy for places that actually need it, and stop fighting a battle that doesn't need to be fought."

Like Robert, Adanna has learned that life plans are far from set in stone: "I graduated in the peak of the [COVID-19] pandemic, and everything that I had carefully constructed went kind of crumbly." Out of business school, she took an internship at a Dutch venture capital firm investing in African start-ups. But the firm "dragged its feet" in hiring her full-time, and she began putting out feelers elsewhere. Once she allowed herself the option of working for an African firm, the opportunities started to click. She's found herself in a role that feels fulfilling, but her expectations were scrambled.

PETER

Peter, too, has confronted others' assumptions about him and his identity, in ways that relate closely to how he answers the first ultimate question. His mother is from rural Idaho, and his father immigrated to the United States from India as a young child, then brought his family around the country as he pursued a military career. Peter describes his father as "very Americanized . . . and integrated very fully into the American kind of ideal. There's no accent. We really have no ties to India, where he's from." When asked his race on demographic forms, Peter usually responds with "Two or more races" or "Other"; but if he has to choose a single category, he says, "I will usually choose white, because I feel like that's what I identify with." He doesn't feel connected to Indian culture or food, and he doesn't know exactly where his father is from. But while he goes by an American name, his given name reflects his Indian heritage—he describes it as "more of a title [that] does impart a certain idea to people." Several weeks before his interview for this book, Peter received an email from human resources "asking me to confirm my visa status, which I'm obviously not on visa. . . . Clearly, they saw my name and thought I was on a visa. . . . It's weird how [my name] can interact and intersect in a way that I don't identify with at all. But you're still defined by those things. . . . I could go full scorched [earth], change my name and just make it legally Peter. But I wouldn't want to do that either, because it is my name." Peter steadfastly refuses to let himself be "defined by those things, whether or not you choose to be."

Peter's conscious rejection of assumptions about his identity gives him freedom to choose his own path, to define himself and why he is here. He is very intentionally open to trying new things and seeing what sticks. He tried sports in school, but when he discovered speech, it sparked excitement: "That was the first time I realized I could be passionate about something." Following this feeling, he tried out theater and art, and soon defined himself as a lover of drama and art as well. He continues to seek that feeling of passion and to refuse to accept the given path, or what Adanna calls the "hamster wheel." He describes this constant discovery and openness: "There are so many people who box their lives into one archetype. [I realized] that I could be more than just one node."

And in that process of self-discovery, Peter learned that he loves attention and that he places high value on his intelligence and potential.

He explains, "I feel like I've always been—and I think Darden is actually really good for me in this sense—I've always been a smarter person in the room, a more creative person. Coming to business school humbled me a little on that, which is interesting. But I still feel like there are things that I can do really well compared to other people . . . I just have a high opinion of myself, I guess."

As you can see, across just five people from the course, we get very different ideas of what comes up when we explore these questions of "Who are we?" and "Who am I?" Part of the power of narrative is to see the world through the eyes of others, to empathetically occupy their unique vantage points and to see how they make sense of it all. Having the context of their "stories," even through such a brief look into their lives, reveals ways in which we might craft our own answers, what we pay attention to (and leave out), and the struggle of writing our own story. While the first part of each of this book's four chapters is very conceptual, theoretical, and "top-down," it is vital to see how this material percolates up from living our lives: what we notice, what we are drawn to, where we struggle, and how we view ourselves. We need to work from both ends, guided by the questions, to make sense of our lives and to be more aware of how we engage with life. We can't make the most of that process if we aren't noticing these core questions and how we shape and answer them. This isn't primarily a theoretical exercise for academics—it is the daily work we do as we shape the kind of life we want and the person we seek to become.

WORKSHOP ACTIVITIES

ACTIVITY 1: Generate your four sentences on "Who are we?"

- What is your answer to "Who are we?" in four sentences? What should definitely be there and what are you willing to leave out?
- What else would you want to include in your answer if you had more time or space?

- How do you know if you have a good answer? What would you look to in order to figure this out—and what kinds of events, experiences, or ideas have led you to your current answer?
- How, where, or when is your answer helpful to you? How, where, or when is it not so helpful?

As you write your sentences, consider the following prompts to help you reflect on your current answer (i.e., your default operating manual):

- What do you expect from other people? If you had a wise friend who could read your "thought bubbles" as you encountered others, what would they notice? Do you assume others will disappoint you and fail to come through when you need them, or do you tend to assume they are reliable and keep their word? Are they there to serve you and do what you ask of them, or is their presence in your life a gift such that anything they do for you is "gravy"—an unexpected kindness?
- What assumptions do you make about other people? Are they generally trustworthy and want to do good, or do you need to be careful, guarded, and reserved until you figure out whether you can trust them?
- Where can you experiment and take some chances—both to avoid some of the worst outcomes of overtrusting and to generate some novel insights that might create better outcomes and experiences for you (and for other people)? What conditions might you change to make it more (or less) likely that they will respond to you with trust, generosity, and support?
- How do your answers change if you think of human nature as flexible and contextual rather than set in stone and always the same? How can this exercise help you be more conscious of the assumptions you are making—and where you can make different ones? What is present in the current environment that might be leading people around you to behave in (for example) a more

cooperative or competitive way, to be more reserved or open? How might you change those conditions to get more of the behavior you seek?

ACTIVITY 2: Generate your four sentences on "Who am I?"

Try the same exercise with "Who am I?"

- What themes or traits stand out as core to you, and what can be left behind?
- Which stories are fundamental to someone knowing you? In other words, which stories would you tell and which can you leave out?
- What stories would family members and friends tell—and how might their telling of those stories be different from your versions? What does that difference tell you about yourself?
- If you step back from the stories, what do we learn about you—and how does that help you (and others) live differently?
- What experiences have had the biggest impact on who you are today, and what do they say about you? How might you incorporate the future, who you aspire to be, the things you are working on and committing to become? What do those hopes, aspirations, and efforts also say about you and who you (as an emerging and evolving person) are becoming?

ACTIVITY 3: Share

Make sure to share your answers with at least one other person—preferably someone you trust to read what you wrote with compassion as well as a healthy willingness to challenge you, to ask good questions, to make you seriously consider possibilities that aren't part of your current answers.

ACTIVITY 4: Reflect

Think in more detail about the gap between the person you are and the person you seek to become. Who do you really want to be (not what job you want or what accomplishments you hope to realize)? How different is that version of you from the person you are right now? What would it take to get you there—and what kinds of things do you need to do in order to move toward that better version of yourself? When is it time to give up on some of your hopes or plans, because they aren't realistic or have lost their luster?

Finally, how do you know if you have good (or good-enough) answers? And what would it take to change your mind—or at least lead you to consider another way of answering this question? If you aren't open to changing your mind or considering other possibilities, then be courageous and acknowledge that you may just be looking for ways to feel better about yourself or stay in your comfort zone, which is fine. As you dig more into this work and spend time talking to others, you may find things that get you to consider new possibilities.

Note, too, that these exercises are also great tools to better understand others. You can use them to infer how other people would answer these questions, at least how they live out their answers, so you can develop a better theory of who they are and what they are likely to do. Taking the time to think this through and being curious about what makes individuals tick can be an invaluable tool for interacting with them; and keep in mind that just as your answers change over time, staying curious about others will also help you update your implicit handbook on them so that you can change how you interact in ways that better serve you and them.

ACTIVITY 5: Personality test

While there are obvious limitations to these tools, some of the personality tests out there can provide some great data and perspective on who you are (and who others are). Take the Enneagram test (see appendix 2, "Resources," for links). Spend time with the results and use them to inform your answer to the "Who am I?" part of this ultimate question. As you think about the Enneagram number you currently associate with the most, are there aspects of your answer that line up with your number? Are there things you would change about or add to your answer to better align with how this test describes you? Are there aspects of yourself (or your Enneagram number) that you dislike or wish were different? How can you use those reactions to make changes in your life and how you show up each day?

The Enneagram doesn't just put you in a "box." Your number isn't fixed, and there is a range of ways to express how you live out your number. Are you a "healthy" 3 or an "unhealthy" 1? How can knowing your tendencies and ways of looking at the world give you insight into why you feel certain things or react in particular ways? Once you are aware of these tendencies, you have options for how to respond. You can shape and grow your current approach in ways that you want and that better serve you and those around you. With intention and effort, you can bring out the healthier aspects of your number and even change to a different number.

Finally, this test can be eye-opening in terms of understanding your views of others. Why do certain people really bother you? The Enneagram helps you see that for each numbered type, there are corresponding numbered types that are more likely to come across as challenging or annoying, and others that are particularly compatible. Rather than being captive to your emotional response, you can use this knowledge to understand why these people affect you as they do, as well as find ways to engage with them that are constructive and creative.

ACTIVITY 6: **Reflected best self**

My colleague, organizational psychologist and business professor Laura Morgan Roberts, has developed a tool, the "reflected best self" exercise, to learn about and from your own strengths.[25]

The basic steps are as follows:

1. Ask a variety of people—colleagues, family members, friends,

teachers, and so on—to share what they see as your strengths, and to include specific examples. A good way to do this is by email, which makes the next step a little easier too. You can also collect positive feedback over time—thank-you notes, performance reviews, and so on—and then ask follow-up questions so you can more fully understand. Roberts gives this example of a follow-up question: "Thank you for noticing X; your feedback made my day! Could you tell me what about my actions seemed to have a specific impact on you? I am trying to figure out what my strengths are so I can continue to make a positive impact at work."[26] Along with asking others, take time to reflect specifically on a success and how your strength helped you achieve it.

2. Organize their responses and look for common themes.
3. Summarize these themes in a description of yourself.
4. Consider how you might build these strengths or use them in areas you haven't yet thought about, whether in work or in another area of your life. Consider as well how you might bring strengths you enact in one setting (e.g., a volunteer organization) into a different one (e.g., with your family or at your office).
5. Do the same for others: Share your observations of others' specific strengths and how they helped achieve a goal or contributed to a success.

CHAPTER 2

WHY ARE WE HERE, AND WHY AM I HERE?

The two most important days of your life are
the day you were born and the day you find out why.
—Commonly attributed to **MARK TWAIN**

What does it mean to be here? To what am I called? What values, traits, and capacities must I embody in my life? These are the kinds of questions that call us out of the trivial, that help us reframe our frustrations and disappointments and step into something larger than fitting in, being successful, being safe, and being accepted by everyone.
—**JAMES HOLLIS**, *Living an Examined Life*

For we carry our fate with us—and it carries us.
—**MARCUS AURELIUS**

The first ultimate question occurs when our human capacity to wonder about the things in our world directs its attention to who's doing the wondering. We wonder about the nature of our world and of people, which leads us to wonder about our own nature and individual identity.

But our capacity for wonder doesn't stop there. We're saddled with a consciousness that has another peculiarity. We are curious about the nature of our world, but we also find ourselves asking about its reasons for being. We want to know what the world is like at any given moment, but we also want to know where it comes from, where it's headed, and what it all means. This second kind of curiosity follows from the first. If we're curious about our world, it's because our curiosity isn't satisfied by immediate appearances or easy answers. We want to go deeper, to imagine what unites those appearances. And we want to know where it all comes from, where it's leading, and how it all has a value or purpose. Questions of "what" lead naturally to questions of "why." And another curious thing happens when that kind of wondering turns to the person asking the question: We become interested in how we're connected to this larger sense of purpose. The very idea of purpose links the person who imagines it to the world they're imagining.

In discussing the first ultimate question, I focused on some of the qualities that make humans distinctive. When we reflect on that question, it can feel like a scientific exercise. Our goal (we might think) is simply to describe the kind of creature we are, just as a botanist's goal is to describe the particular nature of a pine tree or an ornithologist's goal is to describe the distinguishing traits of a blue jay.

But as we saw in the previous chapter, the process isn't merely a scientific one, by which I mean one of objective observation of measurable patterns. When we define who we are, we're describing who we've been, but we're also considering who we want to be. Our human nature is in part the qualities and characteristics we notice in ourselves, but it's also our goals, aspirations, and dreams. My desire to be a caring human is wrapped up in the type of person I am, even if I'm occasionally cruel. Our moral principles can seem like so much deadweight when we consider the atrocities we've committed as a species, but even if we often fall short of our own standards, they influence us and frame our self-judgments; they are a part of who we are. When we consider our "nature," we're also weighing in on what that nature should be. The exercise of thinking through the question isn't neutral: It's shaped by our values and how we look at the world.

And so our first ultimate question sets us up to ask a second one. Our ability to ask who we are reveals a partial capacity to shape the answer, and we shape the answer based on what we think our purpose is. Thinking about who we are leads us to ask why we're here.

WHY ARE WE HERE?

Humans have the capacity to ask "why" about other objects and forms of life—and those whys can have many meanings. We ask why butterflies have all the qualities they have and how they evolved to look and behave as they do now, but we also wonder why they are so beautiful to the human eye. We ask why horses are such good bearers of cargo, but we also ask why they're so graceful, and why they seem to glow when they run in an open field. As these examples make clear, our asking "why" might lead us to answers that are scientific, factual, and utilitarian, but they can also lead us to contemplate the profound, the spiritual, the moral, and the artistic dimensions of things. Part of asking "why" comes from our desire to simply understand the world, to grasp how things work and how they can be of use to us. This skill proved extremely helpful to humans from an evolutionary standpoint. Our abilities to observe patterns, to devise basic causal explanations, and to invent functions for objects (e.g., to create tools) made it much easier for us to survive. Today, when we ask "why," we often limit ourselves to the neutral, scientific, or utilitarian form of the question. We say the earth revolves around the sun because of the effects of gravity, or that money exists to facilitate the exchange of goods. The earth doesn't revolve around the sun because it deserves to; that's just something that, because of gravity, it does. While so many people spend their lives pursuing this thing called money as though it were the most real and important thing in the world, the truth is that it lacks any inherent value: Money is a fiction created to facilitate exchange, and it does so only because humans chose, collectively, to see it as something with value. Even in the early periods of human history, we see humans seeking more than a sparse, factual, utilitarian perspective. From the beginning of language, it seems, people have sought to weave stories out of all the things they encounter, stories that are not only true but beautiful.[1] These fictions allow us to combine our penchant for creativity with our need to create better and more interesting tools, fostering the growth of civilization. And sometimes we create tools and stories so mesmerizing that we have trouble distinguishing what is real from what is simply a human convention.

And so, long ago, groups of people told each other origin stories as they tried to answer their own "Why are we here?" questions. Trees (which, as you'll recall, we considered briefly in chapter 1) figure in many of these origin stories, so we'll use them as an example again here. In Cherokee mythology, the cedar tree was fashioned by the Creator to hold the spirits of those who had died during a long early night.[2] The Buddha achieved enlightenment under a fig tree.[3] The Vikings believed in many worlds, all held by Yggdrasil, the world-containing tree.[4] In ancient Egyptian mythology, the gods and goddesses came into existence under an acacia tree, and an acacia tree enfolded the sarcophagus of the god Osiris and ushered in his rebirth.[5] In the Judeo-Christian tradition, trees are a symbol of life, and in Genesis, Adam and Eve gained wisdom along with shame and pain when they ate the fruit of the tree of knowledge of good and evil.[6]

Trees have been understood throughout human history as having a particular kind of power, and scientists—from climatologists and biologists to psychologists and urban planners—are discovering their importance in ecosystems, climate, and weather. There's evidence not only that they help remove carbon dioxide from the atmosphere, but also that they cool local areas, improve people's physical and mental health, and even increase our longevity.[7] Some scientists are investigating trees' power to communicate with each other and the ecosystem in which they live: Forest ecologist Suzanne Simard writes that trees "are in a web of interdependence, linked by a system of underground channels, where they perceive and connect and relate with an ancient intricacy and wisdom that can no longer be denied."[8]

From prehistory to modern science, then, trees aren't just a thing that *is*; they're also a thing that *does*. They're not just a what, but also a why. They have roles to play, and because of this, they have meanings. We notice, then, that across many cultures, a tree's meaning or purpose exists as part of a larger story.

And that sense of being something larger, a longer and more beautiful story, of being both an object of observation and active creator of that story, is what characterizes our search for purpose and meaning—our why—as well.

In his classic *I and Thou*, philosopher Martin Buber, too, begins with a meditation on a tree: "I contemplate a tree. I can accept it as a picture: a rigid pillar in a flood of light, or splashes of green traversed by the gentleness of the blue silver ground." He considers the tree as movement, as an instance of a particular species, as evidence of physical laws, "but it can also happen, if will and grace are joined, that as I contemplate the tree I am drawn into a relation, and the tree ceases to be an It." For Buber, the shift from "It" to "Thou" is the move toward meaning, the moment in which "one's whole being" is involved in "the cradle of actual life."[9] He finds meaning and purpose in relationship—which we might imagine as an unfolding story involving two (or more) living beings.

From the ancient civilizations to modern philosophers and scientists, people have been telling stories—about trees and everything else—that articulate their sense of connection to each other and the larger world, and that enfold themselves and the things of the world into a system of larger spiritual meaning. And when we turn to how we view our own sense of purpose, we also shuffle between the factual and the (for lack of a better word) spiritual, and we do this by connecting our own stories to larger stories about the universe. We all have purposes, in the sense of goals and motives and drivers, states of the future that we desire and want to bring about. But when those purposes are connected to a larger or longer-term sense of Purpose, it's because we're able to tell a larger spiritual story—about the world, where it's headed, and how our lives contribute to that path.

The Austrian philosopher, psychologist, and Holocaust survivor Viktor Frankl argues that this impulse is fundamental to our nature, that humans are creatures motivated by our search for meaning in life, and that we do it without thinking or consciously choosing to, all day and all the time. To make his point, Frankl drew on his experience as a prisoner in concentration camps during World War II. He found that the capacity to wake up and find a reason to keep going was part of what kept those prisoners who were able to survive in the camps alive, even as they endured the worst conditions imaginable. According to Frankl, it was when someone lost this ability that other prisoners knew they were about to die: "Woe to him who saw no more sense in his life, no aim, no purpose, and therefore no point in carrying on. He was soon lost."[10]

For actor Chadwick Boseman, too, a sense of purpose and principle kept him going after losing a job. As he told the 2018 Howard University graduating class, "When you have reached the hilltop, and you're deciding on next jobs, next steps, careers, further education—you would rather find purpose than a job or career. Purpose crosses disciplines. Purpose is an essential element of you. It is the reason you are on the planet at this particular time."[11]

In contrast to the quote from Mark Twain that begins this chapter, the point is not that people need to understand *the* answer, the singular goal, the one "meaning of life." As Frankl writes, "The meaning of life always changes, but . . . it never ceases to be."[12] This life-sustaining purpose is different for each individual—one person finds meaning in their children and loved ones, another through their intellectual or creative output; one through helping people with special needs, another through their religious vocation; some through creating outstanding products and services that make others better off; and so on. And within each of these large categories, of course, are many individual purposes.

Indeed, you might think of this work of storytelling like archaeologists' sifting through layers of earth to find long-buried treasures. There are many layers of meaning separating us from the past, even as we have the capacity to empathetically try to understand what life was like back then. But all these layers—all these purposes—share one quality: They connect the individual to a story and a community that is larger than the self. Contrary to the *Homo economicus* view I discussed briefly in the introduction, in which people are motivated purely by greed, amassing wealth for wealth's sake is unlikely to give the larger sense of purpose and meaning that, it turns out, is deeply human, even life-sustaining. Of course, money is necessary and helps us access many things we need and want, yet we should not lose sight of the fact that what we really seek are deeper notions of meaning and value that money can symbolize—like achievement, security, freedom, status, or virtue.

There is psychological and biological evidence, too, for the therapeutic effects of finding purpose beyond the self. Volunteering reduces depression among adolescents; a feeling of purpose in life leads to more preventive health care services and fewer nights in the hospital; the ability to find meaning in experience leads to more resilience and faster recovery; employees who feel they are living out their purpose are more engaged and even increase company profits; the studies go on.[13] We are purpose-seeking creatures, so perhaps it should be no surprise that acting from a sense of purpose tends to be good for us and for others.

WHY AM I HERE?

This brings us to the second part of this ultimate question: "Why am I here?" What is my purpose? From what larger calling do I derive meaning?

If we reflect on our own lives and pay attention to the way in which we get through the day, we notice that our internal monologues are filled with small efforts to find or create meaning, and that it's this ability that gets us through experiences that we find boring, painful, or frightening.

Even at this intimate and everyday level, we're looking for more than a factual explanation for our experiences. When we're frustrated by the drudgery of our day job, we're not satisfied by telling ourselves we have to work in order to finish the tasks we've been assigned. When we're training for a marathon, we'd like to know more about the sometimes-horrible exhaustion we feel than that it's caused by an oxygen deficit in our lungs. These explanations might be factually true. They, in one sense, give us answers to the question of "why." But we want something deeper, a meaning that's more meaningful, that provides not just an explanation but a justification—something that connects us to a larger universe of meaning.

What does it concretely mean to connect a sense of individual purpose to a larger system of meaning? How do we go about searching for meaning?

Part of the point of this chapter (and of the process of ultimate questions) is that purpose is inherent to being alive. It is as fundamental as breathing. The interesting questions are which purposes resonate with us and how we can navigate life in ways that help us write better stories, both for ourselves and for our communities. We don't start from scratch in a world that lacks meaning. We begin in the "middle of the story"—in a family, a community, a world in which many meanings are given to us. Our job is to live in that world of meaning and find our place. Some of that involves accepting what is, recognizing that we can't just change the world of meaning on a whim and expect others to follow suit, because so many existing meanings are deeply entrenched in our lives and in social institutions. With luck, we are born into a community with meanings that we find rich, beautiful, and uplifting. Yet, even in the best of societies, many of those meanings include dark and oppressive aspects—a history and a set of shared understandings about life that we may have trouble fully embracing. But within that complex world, we seek our own place, our own life, and a way of living that we find good. The trick for each of us is figuring out what that means in our life, especially in a world where we have so many choices and where society places such a big focus on living out your (individual) purpose.

If purpose, as I've suggested at the beginning of this chapter, links the person who imagines it to the world they're imagining, then maybe one characteristic of the *feeling* of purpose is what Martin Buber conveys in his meditations in *I and Thou*—a feeling of being involved in the "cradle of life," a feeling that we are creators of meaning and stories rather than just the subjects of them. We can find clues to purpose in our own behavior if we just pay attention. We have intrinsic motivators: Even very young children are motivated to help, without the possibility of reward, when they see that someone needs it. Interestingly, when they are rewarded with a treat, they are actually *less* likely to help, which supports the importance of intrinsic, as opposed to extrinsic, motivators.[14] Similarly, behavioral scientists like Mihaly Csikszentmihalyi draw our attention to a state of being called *flow*—which, Csikszentmihalyi holds, is an important answer to the question "What makes people want to go on with the effort required from life?" He defines flow as "a subjective state that people report when they are completely involved in something to the point of forgetting time, fatigue, and everything else but the activity itself."[15] Many people can readily think of activities they do or moments in their lives in which they feel this sense of flow. Yet without this construct to help us reflect on our experiences—without naming the feeling of flow—we often miss the significance of this feeling and the activities that generate it. Csikszentmihalyi reminds us that our bodies and our feelings provide important clues about purpose and what we value. Each of these sources—our thoughts and internal wonderings as well as our lived experience, how we feel—can provide important clues on our path to discovering our purpose and to homing in on the activities, routines, and work that allow us to live it out. Both flow and Buber's sense of "thou" connect to the primal urge to include ourselves in stories we want to tell and live in, like the origin myths I mentioned at the beginning of this chapter.

When you consider your own life, you're likely not considering beings with magical or mythical powers. But you still might take a page from the example of myths. Returning again to Joseph Campbell, we find that myths are powerful stories, found in all cultures, that both reflect and reveal deeper notions of meaning and of our place within the larger system of life.[16] Things like rites of passage, group gatherings and ceremonies, and other kinds of rituals (like, in the United States, reciting the Pledge of Allegiance or singing our national anthem) are part of this collection of meanings embedded in every culture. These rites of passage can endow those who go through them with a sense of accomplishment, of belonging, of becoming someone new—they make up a fundamental component of human culture that seems to be losing power. It may well be that this loss or discounting of rituals and rites of passage is part of the cultural malaise we are experiencing. Myths leave it up to us to pull out a lesson, or a moral, or something even more mysterious, like a sense of larger cosmic harmony and balance. Myths can offer a kind of moral teaching, but they also have meaning as what we might call objects of art. They give the universe sense by connecting it to a set of moral values, but they also give it sense by containing it in a great story, one that's powerful and satisfying on its own, quite apart from the lessons they teach. When we consider our own lives, we also go beyond the simple facts of our personal narratives. As we did with trees, which became—as we contemplated them in myth, science, and philosophy—active parts of their worlds, we too create meaning: We draw out something that makes those facts click into place, that gives them sense, that imparts artistic or spiritual power. In the previous chapter, I suggested that, when we think about who we are and who I am, we're basing those identities on our values and shared fictions. When we think about why we exist and why I exist, we're also drawing on something greater than the mere facts. We're drawing on our own values and even our artistic tastes, which embody and reflect our larger notions of value, to choose and create a story of our own. Thinking about the question means coming up with a kind of story and then drawing out for ourselves what that story means. Purpose is, in part, something we create.[17] It requires a kind of authorship. We take the shared fictions that surround us and make them our own.

All these stories and meanings, cultural and individual and every level in between, are going on around us and through us, all the time. But most of the time, we don't see them or appreciate their importance or the choices we have when we do. Ultimate questions draw our attention to these meanings and the importance they have for us—and for those around us.

As with individual people, every company (and all stakeholders involved) also has an answer to the question "Why am I here?," and this answer shapes the company's behavior, including what other firms it interacts with, how it makes choices, and what it values. Indeed, the last thing a business wants to do is sell you a widget (the very professional business term for a nondescript thing that has some generic notion of value) at arm's length. Instead, businesses want to imbue their products, the experience of interacting with the company, and the larger brand with meaning, with value, with purpose. Why do people go out of their way to buy Apple products? Partly because Apple makes high-quality products at a price many customers are willing to pay. Yet it goes deeper. Apple has cultivated an ethos that borders on mythology. I remember back when I was in graduate school and Apple was starting to become a big thing to the point that it was starting to challenge the existing PC market. Its iconic ad for the 1984 Super Bowl leveraged George Orwell's *1984* to show how Apple represented the forces challenging "Big Brother" and fighting against tyranny. What did that book have to do with choosing between a Mac and a PC? Absolutely nothing in terms of the specifications of the machines and how they performed. Yet it was a brilliant ad that helped shape the brand of the company and sparked its near-cult status among some devoted consumers. People want functionality and efficiency, yet they also want to be linked to stories, values, and kinds of meaning that become part of making and consuming a product. Great brands understand this and actively cultivate it; and when done well, this can foster an incredibly devoted set of stakeholders that sustain the brand and generate new sources of value.

If you see people walking out of a grocery store with their purchases in a Whole Foods bag, are they just using a device that has basic utility for them (carrying their groceries), or are they making a statement about who they are and what they value? If you take a moment to notice it, you will see how much commercials and other forms of advertising incorporate existing meanings that are rooted in societally shared fictions—things like community and connection with others, how a product enhances our health or well-being, and our desire to appear better than others—and how they use those meanings to shape a desirable brand purpose, even if it has little to do with the product for sale. It is also worth looking for the ways in which companies use these meanings to get forms of cooperation from us that, when we step back, seem odd. For instance, how many of us walk around in clothes that proudly display brand logos? If you go to a school, a basketball game, or a supermarket, chances are you will see them all over the place. Customers are, in effect, providing free advertising for companies.

Why do we do this—and for free? Most consumers haven't even thought about it, often because we see the brand as saying something about us, about who we are, that we want to highlight. We also see other forms of odd behavior with companies like Lego that manage to get customers to come in and help them design the next iterations of their products.[18] These customers are, in effect, acting like employees without the pay, benefits, or official titles—and, most importantly, providing invaluable input that creates newer and better products that other customers will want. Sales teams and marketers spend a lot of time trying to see the world through the eyes of their customers. Lego has found a way to take most of the guesswork out of that, and it does so without needing to turn its customers into employees it has to pay.

Companies have built and continue to build relationships with their customers based on their shared purpose. In short, if we look at business through the lens of ultimate questions, we see a whole other dimension that we have been trained to ignore. Business is not primarily about the physics of money—it is about the creation and appropriation of value, which crucially includes meaning and connection. This isn't surprising because business is made up of people, and these questions around purpose are embedded in what it is to be human.

Organizations like businesses can also hijack that need for purpose. They can use a sense of purpose to exploit workers: Finding fulfilling work in which you feel that sensation of flow and that expresses your values is important, but companies can also use workers' desire for meaning to pay them less than their work is worth,[19] or you can find yourself prioritizing your job over your family and health if the firm's mission seems to justify overwork. Similarly, as customers, we may want to support businesses that act as good stewards of natural resources, but firms can fabricate misleading "green" credentials in a process that's become so widespread it has a name: greenwashing.[20]

Still, even more than the individual people who create them, staff them, and keep them running, firms—and their leaders—have an incredible opportunity to highlight how they make others (and the world) better off: Leaning into a larger notion of purpose can animate the firm and get people excited about what it does. This is not a call to proclaim that your company "only does good" or is "serving the planet and its people"—these claims are so huge and unmeasurable as to be meaningless. Such ambiguous and generalized notions of meaning can be only indirectly related to what the firm does, while an effective mission statement plays a genuine and pervasive role in how decisions are made at the company. Leaders looking for a more authentic and consistent sense of purpose in their companies, it turns out, benefit by simply discussing—with openness, vulnerability, empathy, and curiosity—that search with their employees, colleagues, customers, and other stakeholders. These discussions help clarify a firm's purpose, make sure it's grounded in the experiences and individual purposes of the stakeholders, and lead to stronger engagement with and belief in the organization.[21]

As Larry Fink, CEO of BlackRock, wrote in his 2019 letter to shareholders, "Purpose is not a mere tagline or marketing campaign; it is a company's fundamental reason for being—what it does every day to create value for its stakeholders. Purpose is not the sole pursuit of profits but the animating force for achieving them."[22]

If we start with a more human-centered way of thinking about business, where we see the value and meaning embedded in business (and the process of creating that value), we see that every business has an implied purpose—one it lives out regardless of whether that matches the "purpose statement" that almost every firm creates (and which so often has nothing to do with how the firm operates). As one example, I like what Old Dominion Freight Line has done. It could say "We ship stuff" or "We find ways to make as much money as we can by shipping," but instead it says that it is "helping people keep promises." And, if you think about what a shipping company does, it makes sense. Old Dominion's slogan is an aspirational way to think about its work that helps people remember the good that it does for others by being great at what it does. More businesses need to lean into this way of thinking, because people like (and even need) to feel like what they do matters—and because if we make it real and live it out, good things tend to happen for our customers and other stakeholders.

But even companies with statements like this often miss out on the chance to leverage their potential by neglecting to connect the slogan with the vocabulary and behavior of people within the organization. People who have been part of a great team or organization (or a bad one) know that one of the most important contributors to the success and enjoyment of the process is the capacity to create shared meanings and then to live them out—to be able to count on others to "come through" and do the thing that helps the group be at its best, even if that means not being the center of attention or seeking to stand out. Rightly understood, this activity is about trying to make the kinds of meaning that are already embedded in the structure, system, and vocabulary of the company more intentional, systematic, and dynamic.

When a business authentically lives out its purpose, it can believably and persuasively distill a larger story that conveys that into a pithy slogan everyone can understand—for example, "helping people keep promises." A statement like this clarifies and highlights the business's "why" in a way that we often struggle to do in our own lives. When we articulate our shared purpose and the ways in which we need people to collaborate to create it, we unleash incredible power to help people generate value that was previously unattainable.[23] Just as *Homo sapiens* could outcompete Neanderthals because of their ability to create plans and shared fictions, so too can businesses create enormous power when they articulate these deeper notions of purpose and shared value that help people collaborate more intentionally and effectively.

Businesses' purposes are often very explicit, which makes them easy to see. Our own purposes can be harder to tease out.

It is far easier to see purpose when we encounter people and cultures different from our own.[24] "They" aren't like us . . . look at how (and what) they eat, what they teach their children and how they raise them, and the stories they tell about how the world was created and why humans came to be. The fact that the meanings others live with are different from our own helps us to name these as meanings and to see them as human creations that are shaped by human culture and creativity rather than being factual and objective. And looking at other cultures enables us to see the meanings we ourselves live with as our creations, creations that are shapable and shaped by us.

So, if we are paying attention, we see that humans are creatures who find, create, and crave meaning even when we aren't consciously trying to do so. This impulse has bequeathed to us the stories that shape how we see the world and our place in it. But even as we're shaped by the stories we've been given, this tendency also appears in our desire to find our own path and to tell our own story. We seek to know why we are here, and this shows up all over the place in our lives, including in popular culture (think of Billie Eilish's award-winning song "What Was I Made For?" from the *Barbie* movie). Even as we exist in a family, a neighborhood, a community and culture, a civilization, and a history that goes back many thousands of years, as we saw in the last chapter, we still seek to write our own individual stories and imbue our lives with our own meaning. We can't escape those stories or collections of meaning that come to shape our understanding of the world and that mold us into the storytellers that we are. So, as we craft our own purpose, we try to take those existing stories and use them in our own way.

This creates a tension between the public and personal aspects of purpose. The collections of stories in our culture radically shape our understanding. We operate in a world that is already populated by a bunch of existing powerful stories, many of them so familiar that we often fail to notice their influence in everyday life. Those stories can't simply be dismissed or erased, and they're sometimes even enforced—by family members, friends, coworkers, even agents of the state. To escape social pressure, we often mold our stories to fit with the narratives that are already out there. And at a more subtle level, we adjust our stories to make ourselves understood—including to ourselves. If one purpose of our stories is to communicate something about our lives to other people, then the stories have to make sense—they have to be decipherable to a mind shaped by the existing narratives. Charting our purpose is therefore a delicate balancing act. We want to articulate a purpose that's our own, one that's original and unique, but we also need it to harmonize with the stories that already surround us.

As we communicate our purpose to others, we gain more conscious awareness of that purpose, enabling us to consider it, tweak it as we go through life, and more fully embody it. This happens in businesses too—when employees and other stakeholders are committed to a business's mission and purpose, they are more interested in its strategy, more willing to implement it, more motivated to be creative in adapting it to circumstances, and more inspired to continue to uphold shared ideals: "Being able to see business as a force for good, as a place where we create new products and services that people want and see as things that make their lives better (as well as a source of financial return), is essential to creating the conditions under which firms can leverage purpose to drive innovation and performance."[25]

STUDENT VOICES

Having considered some of the ways in which humans create and seek out purpose, let's turn to some reflections from my former students. They provide a more grounded, bottom-up way to see how people deal with the themes of this chapter—and we see in their accounts some ways in which they struggle as well as strategies they adopt to try to realize their goals.

ROBERT

In his description of his purpose, Robert first evokes a desire to give back, which fits with what looks, to an outside observer, like a story about finding a need and helping. After being given a second chance by a judge after his arrest for stealing at age thirteen, Robert decided in college to teach prisoners; after the September 11 attacks on the World Trade Center, he enlisted in the military; and after his brother died of a drug overdose, he got a job at a pharmaceutical company. But as we saw in chapter 1, Robert quickly complicates this simple story, pointing instead to a larger, godlike force: When a parachute accident impaired his fertility, he thought, "What if I was never supposed to have children? Thankfully, I was born and live in a place where there's medicine that can help me in this area. And then hopefully, this is meant to be. But then there's this whole other process of . . . what if I wasn't supposed to [have a child], because the reason I got hurt was I wasn't meant to?" He seems to be gesturing at some larger purpose, but an impersonal one. "I do believe that there is probably something out there guiding us or helping us," he says, but it is also "like a Ping-Pong ball bouncing around into who we ultimately become." He seems to be answering the "Why am I here?" ultimate question with something like a fatalistic or deterministic view.

However he defines it, it is clear that Robert finds ways to be part of and contribute to groups larger than himself. He sees a progression toward greater joining: "I went through this whole evolution as a kid who got made fun of, who wanted to then fit in, to [one who thought] *I don't really care what you think about me*, to then being recruited to join fraternities at William & Mary (and I said absolutely not; I'm not joining a club like this), to then joining the biggest club in the entire United States of America"—the military.

And he frequently cites another source of purpose in his life: his older brother. When they were children, Robert's older brother picked on him; unlike Robert, who had a speech impediment as a young child and was made fun of for his looks, his brother was, in Robert's words, "extremely charismatic, attractive, great with girls, and great in sports," and Robert was "jealous of him my entire life." But in his mid-twenties, Robert experienced what he calls a "role reversal": While his brother retreated into drug addiction and became "just a shell of who he was," Robert "graduated from one of the best schools in the country, got a master's degree, went to law school, was jumping out of planes for the army." And as he talks about his brother, he also points to the power of ambition—to escape his shame over being humiliated by his brother and other kids, he'd imagine a different world in which he fit in and succeeded. He idolized Ronald Reagan, watching every one of his State of the Union addresses before he was even ten years old. He calls curiosity another "driving force" in his life: "I've always been extremely curious about different things. When I don't know why the planetary alignment happens . . . I want to learn about it. I would read physics books for fun because I wanted to know about things I didn't know about."

Robert struggles with how to reconcile these powerful forces in his life: his brother's influence on the one hand and his own ambition, curiosity, and urge to help people on the other. "The overwhelming drive of ambition and curiosity, combined with the passion to make a difference" have guided him in all his choices, he explains. But then he switches the narrative and brings up a line in Radiohead's song "Paranoid Android" about ambition's ugliness. He reflects, "I've kind of juggled that line in my head for two decades now, and yes, I agree. I kind of wish I wasn't as ambitious. However, it drives other productive philanthropic good things in the world for sure. Just today, I had a lunch meeting about being a board member for an $800 million endowment."

JOSHUA

As you'll recall from chapter 1, Joshua found his identity through finding his voice. He began to see himself as the author of his own story when he learned how to honor all the parts of his identity: grandson of a change maker, Black man, cybersecurity expert, basketball player, Darden graduate, and more.

There were obvious structural obstacles to professional success for a Black man in Joshua's field. They appeared as the subtle patterns, policies, and practices that worked to minimize the presence and visibility of Black men in the cybersecurity industry, especially in leadership. But they also worked from the inside out, seeding themselves into Joshua's sense of self and eroding his belief in his abilities. When he entered the industry after graduation from college, he says, "it was a struggle to feel like I had any value. Some of the team was like, 'Man, this guy knows nothing.' I didn't feel like I deserved to be there."

These barriers might have been overpowering. But as he's crafted his story, Joshua has recast them as fuel for a sense of purpose. Faced with exclusion, Joshua has forged a personal mission that's both self-empowering and generous. He has cultivated a sense of confidence by slowly achieving tangible accomplishments that secure his sense of self.

It's allowed him to claim "a place at the table," and to develop connections with friends and colleagues who also "excelled at being button pushers." These friends and acquaintances have taught him a lot: "I'm learning from this huge representation of people . . . and I do find it incumbent upon me to take and embody that and give back, so that very much is interwoven into [my] purpose. It's not for me to take it and use it solely for myself." After experiencing exclusion, he says, "my purpose boils down to being a developer and connector. A developer of people, showing people, especially those on my team or who report to me, that there's so much opportunity and impact that they can make in their careers, even if they feel like they can't do something. [I let them know that] I have confidence in them, that it's not going to be easy, but it's something they can do. I embody the same struggles and hurdles that they had. [They can see] the 'success'"—he puts air quotes around *success*—"I've had, and let that be encouragement that they can do it too. Because if I can do it, you can do it."

He took the story of his grandfather, which itself fits into the larger story of individuals fighting injustice not just for themselves but for all those in their communities and beyond, and made it his own: "I definitely have tried to take, as part of my purpose, to be a button pusher, to break down those barriers in corporate America, and challenge the status quo. And to break those barriers in the community setting. To challenge the status quo to say, 'Black man, Black woman, you have a seat at the table to make an impact in cybersecurity. See yourself in that.'"

So Joshua takes this purpose, this story that reflects and speaks to and is part of a larger story, specifically to his work: "My management style is . . . we're going to be a team, and I'm going to assume positive intent . . . I'm going to look out for you, and I'm going to hope that you see that and that you're going to look out for me, and that we can have a highly cohesive team." This vision fits with his personal and societal mission: "It seems like a far stretch that we'll be able to walk hand in hand like Martin Luther King Jr. mentioned. But I take it upon myself to truly be that catalyst."

LINIKSHA

In her journey inward after immigrating to the United States from India, Liniksha began to practice meditation regularly. When she made the decision to finally break ties with her abusive mother, she experienced a feeling of profound disorientation, which she finally resolved when she "meditated on the beach one day and cried for hours." That experience of disorientation and meditation—along with her journey from abused daughter in India to independent woman in the United States—led her to more fully live in the contradictions. "I'm a victim, and a survivor, and I'm a perpetrator, all three at the same time. I am poor and I'm rich, and I'm in between." And this also led her to quantum mechanics, which, she describes, "allows you to live in a world which is this and that [at the same time], as opposed to what we like to do where it's this *or* that."

She decided to follow her curiosity about quantum mechanics, and she is finding her purpose there too, dwelling in its contradictions: "So, people have explored what else is out there. It led to colonization, didn't it? That question is still being asked—it's within all our hearts—'What else is out there?'" Curiosity, contradiction, colonization—"For me, I want to understand all that. Where are we in time and space? And I want to contribute to that somehow. I think the voices that have contributed to the expansion of our understanding of our world have been primarily men, first of all, and [in the] postcolonization world, white men. And I think that a voice like mine should be at the table, [talking] about the expansion of the world."

She sees great possibilities in quantum mechanics: "If we were able to capture a quantum state in a computer, then I want to know what that means for humanity, for climate change, for everything. And the reason I think that draws me into it is that the more I learn about quantum mechanics, [the more] I know that the phenomena we're barely scratching [the surface of] are experienced in meditation. So, I feel like I have experienced the phenomenon that I'm reading in these books. And so that's why I'm like, 'Wait a minute. I think I might have a perspective here!' Maybe I can push this a little bit. There's not a blazing confidence that I'm going to change [quantum computing]. It's a curiosity, but it's a continuous curiosity. It does not take energy for me. It gives me energy, and that's the thread that I'm trying to follow."

This may not read as a fully baked notion of purpose, and that's okay—Liniksha's purpose is in process. She is at the beginning of the path that she needs to be on to find and define her purpose, and she feels that beginning, that "continuous curiosity."

ADANNA

After Adanna graduated from college, she got a job where she felt like she was just one small part in a huge, impersonal company; she had no way to know what her impact was on the larger world: "My first job was [at] a big investment bank with thousands of people. You're working on this Excel spreadsheet, and you don't know how it feeds up to the wider community, and every time I'd try to understand the wider picture . . . something just didn't quite fit."

She quit her job and moved back to her home country. "When I went back, . . . it was the first time in my life where I was making what I described as an active decision." This was a key inflection point in her life, a switch from what felt like a predetermined path to one she chose. "Everything has always had a process: You finish primary school, you go to university, you get a job. And that was the first time where I was choosing to quit something. It was a weird time, where I had to really think, *Okay, I'm not going to stay on this hamster wheel.*" At the same time, her friends—the cohort with whom she'd run those years on the hamster wheel—were also making their own choices, so this marked an inflection point in her social life as well: "People are figuring out their own jobs, so it's the time in your life when people stop being on the same track as you." This was, as it is for so many of us on this hamster wheel, an opportunity to think more consciously about ultimate questions.

She decided to return to school to earn an MBA, which she describes as another "very introspective period." As part of that introspection and questioning, she gained clarity about her "why": "What's always been important is leaving everyone, everywhere better than I found it. I just want to have a positive impact. When people think about me, they think about how I made them feel positive, feel a personal impact I had on the work we were doing."

And after earning her MBA, she did not return to the impersonal world of corporate banking, where she might have been proud of her hard work but felt unmoored without an idea of what effect it was having on actual people. Instead, she joined a financial technology (fintech) firm in Africa, a company whose mission made even the most mundane task feel impactful: "I feel very fulfilled here on almost every single thing I work on. It can be the most mundane task in the world, like physically finding documents, and I know why I'm doing it, so I never feel like I'm just wasting away. I know how much impact I'm giving to every single thing I'm working on. And [the company is] small enough that at least people recognize your impact as well." The firm's mission is to support very small businesses in Africa. Before going to business school, Adanna had not heard of this kind of work: "This company wasn't on my radar and this industry wasn't on my radar. It's an online payments company. And in the African continent, that's very new. Ninety percent of businesses are just microentrepreneurs. They're just trying to sell things day to day, and they're not able to get a lot of customers until they go online. That's what unlocks opportunity." Believing in the company's mission and understanding the need for her work, Adanna not only knows she's making a difference; she trusts that even when she's not aware of her exact impact, it's still there: "I'm still making the difference that I wanted without even realizing it."

PETER

Peter, too, rejects predetermined paths. In refusing to let others define him, he prioritizes new experiences and new opportunities by constantly cultivating his passions and seeking new ones.

He designed a board game: "That entrepreneurial endeavor, this act of creation, is super important to me. It really fuels me and gives me fire. This idea that I can make something that makes someone else's life better: That's what I just want to keep striving for in my life."

He plans to have children: "I'm very excited for later on down the line, because I [will] have a huge impact as just one person with this little person."

But he also wants "influence and money": "I think I've always felt very small, because I'm just one person. . . . It's kind of like the one-voter scenario in politics, right? It's my one vote. Is it really going to count? I'm just one person: What's my impact? So . . . I want to have a bigger, broader impact."

With interests in creating and creativity, in nurturing, and in making an impact on the world, Peter wants to translate his enthusiasm into leadership and change: "I want to make a difference. I want to stand out. I want to do something in the world that actually effects change, and that's why I try to aspire to positions of leadership, always aspiring for more." While he continues to define and redefine himself and why he is here, Peter knows that he needs to connect that with something larger than himself even if he hasn't fully figured out where or how he will do it. He has the building blocks of purpose, yet he needs more time and experience to realize what that asks of him and what kinds of things he might do to "make a difference" that feels right to him. Peter is searching for the things that allow him to know in his bones, *This is me at my best.* He wants to channel all his energies into doing what feels natural and fulfilling, in service of something that fits with his talents while making a difference beyond himself.

Across these stories we find people in various states of finding and living out their purpose. Each of them is asking "Why am I here?" in some way, and trying on things that may help them answer it. This is normal and healthy. Part of purpose is the process of seeking. Even once we think we have it figured out, we may struggle to keep it burning brightly, or to keep a meaningful connection to it—and we may decide to change what our purpose is or how we define it. We can read the words of our stated purpose, but we may not feel that what we do really lives it out. This is a lifelong struggle—so it's all the more important to be aware of it, to get a sense of how others struggle with it, and to become more intentional about figuring it out and keeping it alive.

WORKSHOP ACTIVITIES

ACTIVITY 1: Generate your four sentences on "Why are we here?"
Try the same four-sentence exercise as in the last chapter with this question: In four sentences, answer "Why are we here?"

- What is essential to your answer and what can be left out—or deferred to when you have more time to answer this question?
- Does anything surprise you about your answer?
- Make sure you talk to at least one other person and get their feedback on what you wrote. What resonated with them? What did they find less important or missing from your answer?
- Where does this answer matter?
- How might having a different answer lead to some different life choices or behaviors? Try to find at least one person to talk with who has a significantly different answer than you and talk about why it's different—as well as how or where your answer matters in your life.

ACTIVITY 2: Generate your four sentences on "Why am I here?"

Now shift to the "I" version:

- Why do you think you are here?
- What helps you sift through all your traits, talents, and experiences to have a sense of why?
- Is there something in your gut, your heart, your mind, or your soul that tells you, "This is why I'm here"?
- Is there an activity (e.g., serving others, being a teacher) that is key to your purpose?
- Are there things you can learn from others to help you?
- If you don't feel like you have a strong or clear sense of why you are here, how does that feel, and how does it impact your approach to life?
- Are you just going through the motions, doing what others do (or expect you to do), and not fully engaging with life? How might life be different if you had a deeper sense of purpose?
- What might you do to build or find a deeper sense of purpose?
- What do you want to say to your future self—the you who is fifteen or twenty years in the future? What would you like to be true about that future you, and what would it require of you to get there? What might that future self say to you now? What priorities would that future self say you need to have, and what choices would they say you need to make, to stay aligned with your purpose and not get off track? What are the mistakes you need to avoid that you might otherwise make?
- If you give up the idea that purpose is like a lightning bolt that hits you out of nowhere (or never hits you), what might you try to better connect with a sense of meaning and purpose? Keep in mind that research shows that when we add external motivators (like money or some other kind of reward), intrinsic incentives sometimes lose power.[26] Build a set of tools and techniques that can help you revisit your purpose as well as assess whether you

are living it out. If purpose isn't singular or set in stone, then we need to cultivate a way of navigating life that helps us to retain or regain our sense of purpose.

ACTIVITY 3: The "why" exercise

To find your answers to why you are here, Wharton School professor Adam Grant suggests the following exercise.[27] First, make a list of things you're passionate about—family, a service activity, a hobby, a research question, a creative pursuit: You decide. Then ask yourself why each one is important to you. Once you have answered the "why" about one activity, ask "why" again about the same activity, and continue until you have no more answers to the why. For example, if you've listed scuba diving as something you're passionate about, you might answer the sequence as follows:

Why? Because I like being underwater.

Why? Because it's so different from my regular life.

Why does that matter? Because I get a new perspective on the world.

Why does that matter? Because I value looking at things in new ways.

Why? Because that's how I grow as a person.

Why does that matter? Because I value personal growth.

This is a process of drilling down into what you value until you find what Grant calls the "core value." It could be personal growth as in the example above, or helping others, or learning, or creating something new, for example—whatever it is for you. Then, once you've identified your core values, you can find other ways, beyond your initial list, to enact and embody them.

You can also do this at work. Once you've identified your core values, you can find ways to bring them into your job. One way to do this is to simply be more intentional about your existing responsibilities: If you value responsiveness, for example, then the process of answering emails is transformed from tedium into meaningful connection. Another, more involved way is to advocate for yourself at work by adjusting your tasks and responsibilities in what Grant calls "job crafting." That can start with a new side project, for example, or a learning group with colleagues.

If you are a leader or manager, you can also help employees do this, simply by asking why they like what they like, and then being open to creative ways to help them do more of what they really value.

CHAPTER 3

WHAT IS THE GOOD LIFE, AND WHAT IS MY GOOD LIFE?

You have to realize that happiness is not something you find at the end of the road. You have to understand that it is here, now.
—**THICH NHAT HAHN**,
You Are Here: Discovering the Magic of the Present Moment

The art of being wise is the art of knowing what to overlook.
—**WILLIAM JAMES**

You have to love. You have to feel. . . . And when it happens that you are broken, or betrayed, or left, or hurt, or death brushes near, let yourself sit by an apple tree and listen to the apples falling all around you in heaps, wasting their sweetness. Tell yourself that you tasted as many as you could.
—**LOUISE ERDRICH**, *The Painted Drum*

The chance to talk about the good life is one of the biggest draws of the "Ultimate Questions" course. We all wonder about the good life and seek it out implicitly. Whether or not we're aware we're doing it—not to mention our ideas of what "the good life" means and our plan for realizing it—this drive toward a good life is in us. And, while most of our focus is on the *good* of our good life, meaning we aim to do positive things, part of the conversation is making sure we avoid big mistakes that can derail our plans—like doing something that's criminal or that brings disgrace. We need to reckon with our darker side and our blind spots to decrease the chances that they'll derail us and prevent us from realizing our good life.

We were all brought into this life without a choice. Yet, as we become aware of being alive and what it means to be human, most of us want to make the most of it. We want to be fully human, to feel present, to experience all the joy and love and excitement that life has to offer.

While we tend to focus on all the good things we want, along the way, we learn the power of sorrow, loss, and struggle. While such "negative" experiences sting and often leave us sad, they bring us something very valuable, and they show us powerful aspects of being human. We learn about ourselves through hardship; we bond more deeply with others by sharing pain; we rejoice in a victory more after the bitterness of a defeat; and we feel the joy of loving another more deeply only after our hearts have been broken.

What do you want your life to be? You may want to start a family, or see the world, or learn how to dance, or sing, or paint. You may want to serve your community quite apart from what you accomplish in your career. You may want the experience of aging gracefully. Or the full adventure of having children: the intensity of those first few years, the years of adolescence and high school when parents question the sanity of ever wanting children in the first place, and the period of heartbreak when they leave home and start their own lives. You may want to care for your own parents and your siblings. You may want to enjoy a life of work (whether at home or in the office) and then start a new chapter in retirement, before you get old and experience your body and mind declining.

That's a lot. Living a good life is about having some idea or plan for how to go about all this, knowing you don't have the time or resources to "do it all" and that you will inevitably have to revise and update that plan. The particular things you want at an earlier point in your life are likely different from the particular things you want at a later point in your life. On top of all that, despite our best intentions, life has a way of veering in unexpected directions, of throwing curveballs that can take us off course and sometimes in very different directions than we intended. Can we roll with the changes and find another way forward with a new vision for our good life, or will this new course leave us feeling lost, bitter, and defeated?

This chapter is about stepping back to think more consciously about how to approach our own lives. My goal here is not to try to turn you into a philosopher or formalize a systematic vision of the good life. It is to help you become more aware of how you are already approaching the good life and to share some insights and resources that can help you enhance your quest for living a good life. We have one shot at life. We want to be able to say (and believe) that we lived it well. That we did our best. That we made the most of our time and our talents. That we had fun. That we did things that mattered. We need certain tools and techniques to adapt on the fly, so that we aren't just stuck with a view of the good life that we will one day come to realize isn't what we're really after.

But the good life is a tricky concept. Even when we carefully consider our ideas of it and perfectly follow through on them, we may not end up with genuine happiness or that deep certainty, that feeling in our bones, that we are living well. You may find that what you thought was the good life is actually dull, exhausting, and tedious, even though you designed it. Maybe the best vision of living a good life I could come up with—with all the plans, mantras, exercises, and twelve-step formulas needed to achieve it—wasn't for me. We can have clear ideas about the good life that we created and still find out we were wrong.

We have the experiences of our elders to remind us of this. Many people get to the end of their lives and realize how foolish they were when they were younger. They realize that happiness was within their grasp, but they let it escape. They got caught up in activities they thought would make them happy but didn't. Some focused too heavily on making money or climbing the corporate ladder and lost sight of relationships and family. Others were too dedicated to relationships and family and had so conformed to the expectations and examples of others that they neglected to live life for themselves. Many people reach old age only to discover a profound sense of disappointment. Only then do they see what would have made their lives rich, but those insights have arrived too late.

In fact, people make predictable mistakes about happiness and the good life: They misidentify what allows human beings to truly flourish. As "happiness hacker" Penny Locaso found after a set of experiments and over a hundred interviews, "the three greatest barriers to leading a fulfilled and happy life seemed to be distraction, fear, and a lack of curiosity about oneself, others, and the world in general." Those who were fulfilled were not happy all the time, but they accepted and appreciated their experiences, enabling them to "lean into uncertainty, embrace emotions (both positive and negative), and adapt to their environment with intention and meaning."[1] Regrets aren't the enemy; they can teach us important lessons and provide opportunities to grow. Of course, this doesn't mean we should seek out opportunities to regret! It means it's important to be willing to do things that are hard, where you might fail, where you take a chance because you want to be bold and experience something of value. Regrets remind us that doing hard things, taking risks, and stretching ourselves are integral to living well. Despite their bad reputation, regrets can be a pathway to understanding ourselves and how we can move toward becoming the person we seek to be.[2]

I don't have a one-size-fits-all version for what counts as the good life. Indeed, if you hear that from someone else, I encourage you to be highly suspicious of whatever they tell you. I can't give you the definitive answer, the one that these disappointed elders learned too late, in part because each person has their own concept of the good life as well as their own judgment as to whether they are actually living that life. As you might expect, given the importance of the question, there is an entire library of ideas related to it. I will cite some sources and provide resources for further reflection, but recounting and summarizing all the wisdom on this topic is a task far beyond what I can do here. Instead, I will touch on a few thinkers who have come before us whose reflections I think are especially relevant, both for generating ideas about the good life and for crafting strategies that can help us live lives we experience as "good."

WHAT IS THE GOOD LIFE?

According to the Greek philosopher Aristotle, the nature of human happiness, flourishing, and well-being—various translations of the Greek word *eudaemonia*, which here we might interpret as "living a good life"—is determined by the kind of beings that humans are.

We might imagine this first by focusing on a nonhuman creature. My Labrador retriever's joy is determined by his "dog-ness" and, more specifically, his "Lab-ness": He seems most fully alive when he is running in the fields with other dogs, chasing rabbits, or swimming in a pond. Those are the activities that draw on his particular canine aptitudes, his "nature." He's a hunter and an explorer. His body equips him for those tasks, he seeks them out without being told to do so, and he derives what looks like happiness from performing them. His instincts, desires, and joys (if we can anthropomorphize a dog) give shape to the kind of good life that "fits" him (as well as other Labs). While we can have a general understanding of a good life, what we need is to make sure that our design fits us—and not another kind of creature. The good life for a Lab is not a good life for a human.

Even less familiar, we might consider, again, a tree. In Martin Buber's contemplation of a tree, once he progresses beyond the "it" of a tree's wood or leaves or greenness, he sees the tree as a thriving, living being in all its complication and immensity: "Everything, picture and movement, species and instance, law and number included and inseparably fused. Whatever belongs to the tree is included: its form and its mechanics, its colors and its chemistry, its conversation with the elements and its conversation with the stars—all this in its entirety." Buber's tree is not its parts or uses (not its "work"), "but the tree itself."[3] It is doing uniquely tree things and drawing them into unity.

These nonhuman examples give us useful context for thinking about a fairly complex idea. For Aristotle, the good life is tied to human nature.[4] We first need to understand the kind of beings we are—the abilities, desires, and skills that are part of what it means to be human (like what we explored in chapter 1). For Aristotle, that task focuses on knowing what human "excellence" looks like and then cultivating our capabilities, which for him draw us to our character. We each seek to become a good person, not just someone who sometimes does good things. Traits that are positive for a dog or a tree are unlikely to also suit a human. So how we describe human nature ends up being critical for identifying what it means to "live well." And once we identify uniquely human nature, we gain happiness and fulfillment from becoming a good person, from developing virtue and making the most of our abilities. That takes intention and effort, as well as time. Just as an athlete requires lots of practice, coaching, and hard work to become great at their sport, humans must actively and intentionally develop virtue. Otherwise, an individual act is just a single data point that doesn't really tell me all that much about who you are or what I can expect you to do in the future.

Happiness is tricky and paradoxical. Aristotle argues that we tend to get it wrong, especially when we aim directly at it by trying to do things that make us feel good in the moment—eating lots of delicious food, drinking alcohol or taking drugs that can create feelings of euphoria, making lots of money, seeking and experiencing sexual pleasure. All these can create momentary joy or a feeling of happiness, yet the more we pursue them, the less fulfillment we find. They can even become obsessions or addictions that make us miserable—we end up in a bottomless pit of always seeking yet never finding a lasting feeling of happiness. The more we seek it out intentionally and directly, the further we find ourselves from happiness.

Instead of trying to maximize pleasure, we get at eudaemonia indirectly. We need to understand our nature and cultivate excellence in who we are. And this process is not just a set of acts that we do; it is a way of being. Virtues are habits, things that I tend to do and that others who know me would expect me to do because I'm that kind of person. My actions over time reinforce the idea that this is who I am—and you would expect me to do similar things in future situations like this. While this can sound esoteric and academic, the focus here is entirely practical and can have great consequence for us: Are you likely to tell me the truth or hide things from me, especially when doing so benefits you? If you are operating on my child, can I trust you to follow my wishes? If I'm going into battle with you, can I depend on you to have my back even if that means putting your own life in danger?

For Aristotle, this work is all about understanding the "virtues" of how we express and live out our nature. For each of our instincts and drives, there is a healthy, or virtuous, way to express it and an unhealthy, or "vice"-based, pattern of behavior. For instance, if I see someone bullying a fellow student who is younger than them (and me), I have at least a couple of options: I can react with courage and try to find a way to protect the kid, even if it puts me in danger, or I can react with cowardice by either ignoring the situation or encouraging the bullying.

Cultivating the virtues and steering away from vices is how we work our way toward being good people. And according to Aristotle, we enjoy being virtuous even when it is hard and may require great sacrifice. Having the discipline to cultivate virtues leads us to enjoy our lives and the things we do. The marathon runner can run over twenty-six miles at a clip—and savor the experience—only because they have committed to the discipline and the hard work it takes to become that kind of elite athlete. Virtue, in some sense, is its own reward—we feel good and we feel like we are excelling in becoming a virtuous person—throughout the process, not just in those moments when we do some great deed like win a race, save a life, or provide wise counsel.

At the same time, cultivating Aristotelian virtues isn't just good for us as individuals; it also tends to make us act in ways that benefit those around us and the larger community. We want people of integrity in our communities because we can rely on them to speak the truth and keep their word. Those patterns of behavior show me that you are likely a good person, one who has consciously cultivated this habit and one I can count on to behave in ways that also benefit the group. Things like collaboration and working together become much easier when we know we're working with people who will keep their word. From the perspective of cultural evolution, we want people who are brave because we need people who will stand up and resist the aggression of a rival community intent on taking our land and resources and enslaving our people. Having people who are virtuous makes it much more likely that the people of our community can live good lives rather than face abuse, tyranny, poverty, and other things that make a good life seem far more elusive.

Of course, Aristotle was not the only one with good ideas about the good life. Many centuries later, utilitarian philosophers Jeremy Bentham and John Stuart Mill shifted the focus away from individual virtue and toward choices that tend to create positive outcomes (pleasure, or what they called *utility*) and avoid negative outcomes (pain) for as many people as possible.[5] Part of the shift toward this approach to ethics and the good life was a response to things like an increased focus on individuals (not just elites) and their inherent worth, living in bigger societies with large institutions, the presence and growth of significant inequality, and the growing awareness that large portions of the population lived in abject poverty. Bentham and Mill wanted to improve the lives of all people—not just those with the resources, time, and privilege to cultivate virtues. After all, Aristotle wrote for a comparatively small community where there was a focus on elites guiding and directing life in the polis. Many have criticized his ideas because they tended to be available only to wealthy landowning male citizens. Enslaved people, women, and most men (in other words, the vast majority of the population) were simply not able to become virtuous in the way Aristotle discussed. While advocates of virtue ethics have good ideas about how the Aristotelian view can address such criticisms, it is useful to leave that framework to get a new perspective. As society became larger, more complex, and more democratic, there was a growing understanding that all people, not just the aristocratic few, matter, and so the utilitarians focused on things that make a tangible difference in the lives of many others: good nutrition, reliable housing, clean water, freedom from prejudice, and access to opportunity. These are much more about social conditions, institutions, and impersonal choices than about who any given individual is or what virtues they have (or lack). Bentham and Mill recognized how hard it is to have a good life when you experience lots of pain and hardship and comparatively little benefit. As a result, they thought our primary focus should be on creating conditions where people face less pain and suffering and have more positive outcomes—things we can measure and even (sometimes) have objective standards for. That way our judgments depend not on gauging someone's inner state of being (i.e., whether they have virtue), which is often difficult to discern, but on things we can measure (e.g., whether they have enough food to eat and a job or income that can sustain them and those who depend on them).

A common critique of this utilitarian focus on outcomes is that we may be led into bad habits—cutting corners, breaking rules, eroding key relationships—that can stain our character and make it harder for us to do the good we want to in the world. For example, if I am willing to break a promise, people will stop seeing me as trustworthy, and they will seek to work with someone else, which diminishes my ability to generate positive outcomes. That said, doing things in the world that make others (and ourselves) better off continues to be an influential and enduring way to think about the good life—or at least a key component of it.

It is interesting that despite this difference in approach, Aristotle also notes that suffering, loss, and tragedy can erode your ability to have a good life. Aristotle, Bentham, and Mill all focus on the "good" part of the good life—things like virtue, pleasure, and happiness—just with very different ideas of what "good" means and how we know if we have it.

By contrast, Viktor Frankl (whom I mentioned in the previous chapter) didn't just acknowledge that pain and loss can impede happiness—he thought that both good and bad experiences were necessary. For Frankl, the good life is about finding (or better yet, creating) meaning, even during the darkest chapters of our lives: This is what makes life worth living, and what makes us human. He argues for a "tragic optimism," meaning the ability "to creatively turn life's negative aspects into something positive or constructive."[6] Our struggle to understand how all the pieces of our lives fit together—and to make them fit in a way that helps us grow—is at the root of our existence. We can give up a lot in life and still make sense of things even when they are dark and painful. But when we give up the sense of authorship that enables us to connect the pieces of our lives together and to something larger than ourselves, all we have left are passive experiences that numb and distract us. A good life is out of reach until we can regain that capacity for making meaning out of life and being open to new ways of finding it.

Martin Seligman, considered one of the founders of positive psychology, developed his theory of well-being after studying trauma, learned helplessness, depression, and other objectively bad experiences. His conception of human flourishing involves five elements: (1) positive emotion—"the pleasant life" filled with happiness along the lines of Bentham and Mill's utility; (2) engagement, or flow—that feeling of being lost in an activity that Csikszentmihalyi explored, as I brought up in the last chapter; (3) a sense of meaning, or connecting your efforts to something greater than yourself, which Frankl highlights; (4) accomplishment—which some might pursue for money or power, but many work toward as an expression of their skill and virtue, as Aristotle advocates; and (5) positive relationships with other people, which Seligman emphasizes especially. Bringing these ideas into the scientific and clinical world, Seligman conducts empirical research and advocates for therapeutic applications to help people, from schoolchildren through the military, live their good lives.[7]

In this section I have tried to give you a sense of how some influential figures have thought about the good life, as well as some of their insights into how humans often end up going off track. Both sets of ideas are important if we want to get closer to our good life. Aristotle argues for individual self-improvement; Bentham and Mill for societal change to reduce pain and increase pleasure, especially on a group level; Frankl for creatively transforming inevitable suffering into meaning and new growth; and Seligman for a kind of synthesis of all of these. These are only a handful of the many thinkers who have taken on the question of what it means to live the good life—whether that means focusing on finding happiness, meaning, fulfillment in life, or some other metric (like living a life of service). I've drawn on these authors because they give us a variety of useful ways to think about the question "What is the good life?" At the same time, they provide a starting place to think about the narrower question of "What is *my* good life?" We can use their ideas to turn from the general question of human thriving to the more particular question of how we understand it and achieve it for ourselves.

WHAT IS MY GOOD LIFE?

You might feel a bit at sea in thinking about the good life; there is a range of ways to understand it that, in turn, shape how you live your life. I don't expect you to have figured it out based on the brief survey of ideas we just covered. Chances are it will take time, reflection, and even experimentation to figure out what truly resonates with you. In the meantime, this chapter provides you with some tools and insights on how to avoid getting derailed or sucked into dead ends when it comes to living a good life. Better yet, this chapter also provides some skills to cultivate that can bring you closer to your own vision of the good life—both what it means and how you can make choices that bring your life closer to that vision.

This is a great place to pause and reflect on your existing answer—how you have approached the good life and what implicit set of priorities or choices you are living your life by. What are you prioritizing? What do you see as most important to do, to invest in, to give your time and talents to? What do you want others to say about you and see in you? We all have an implicit theory and story we are living out. This is the time both to understand your current theory and to figure out ways in which you can learn from others to move toward a way of thinking and living out the good life that is more truly yours, one that you think is worth living for, perhaps even dying for. I want to help you bring out your best thinking and all your experience of life so far—what do you truly love, or hate? What gives you an enduring sense of meaning and value, and what doesn't? Perhaps as important as your own self-reflection is what your friends and those close to you would say about what you prioritize, what you value, what shapes and defines your (implicit) good life. Their input can bring you a healthy perspective on what they see as your answers and how well you are living them out. Your answers to these questions (as well as others' perspectives on those answers) will give you important insights that can help move you closer to living *your* good life.

As you try to achieve the good life for yourself, you might see your progress toward it as a kind of strenuous activity that you must pursue every single day. This approach aligns with the doctrines of Aristotle, who saw human flourishing as the active cultivation of those skills that make us human. To bring his philosophy to the individual level, he might have each of us build the habits that develop the particular skills we were born with: You flourish by actively cultivating the virtues in a way that draws on and accentuates your natural excellences—those traits and abilities that are specific to you and that you want to highlight in how you live your life. If you are naturally skilled at oratory and cultivating wisdom, you might want to pursue life as a teacher or politician—outlets for expressing your abilities as well as allowing you to do things you enjoy.

Or, as you embark on your quest to define and find the good life, you might take a radically different approach. You might try to cram your life—and the lives of as many others as possible—with as many good feelings and experiences as possible, which can, but doesn't have to, involve cultivating your talents. This approach aligns with the utilitarians, who see the good life as about finding ways to create as much good as we can in the world (through, for example, making new products and services that make others better off, or saving lives, or helping people learn to love and care for themselves) while also minimizing harm (by keeping people from being harmed or harming themselves; limiting the risks or dangers of products and services; finding ways to decrease pollution, drug use, or exposure to toxic chemicals; or more). This view puts lots of emphasis on actions and the outcomes of those actions, and much less on you as an individual or on how your actions reflect who you are.

Then again, you might see your life neither as an activity to practice nor as a feeling to pursue, but as a work of art or a novel. Your challenge is to discern, in the life you've led, the narrative arc, or the sense of proportion and balance that distinguishes, say, a great painting. You shape your life by letting yourself be "in the moment" and trusting that those instincts you feel will lead you to the life you seek. Even as you try to live well and have mostly good experiences, you construct an idea of your life that takes in and builds on everything, the good and the bad. You follow your passion and find ways to make meaning out of whatever comes your way, believing that being yourself and listening to your inner voice will lead you toward your best life. This approach aligns more with Frankl and the idea that meaning and joy follow from being attuned to the moment and living it fully.

In all these ways of framing the good life, we want our lives to be filled with activities and experiences that showcase the best in us. We want to feel good and to be happy even if that includes setbacks, sadness, and grief. We want to learn from the bad things that will inevitably happen in our lives. We want jobs that are worth our efforts, and time and resources to do the other things that matter to us. We want our lives to have meaning and value in their fullness, even during—or as a result of learning from—those moments when we feel bad or fall short of our own standards.

We can take a page from each of the thinkers we've discussed as we consider how to achieve the good life on our own. But as we move from *the* good life to *my* good life, we run into the challenge of how to apply these ideas in our own individual ways. Part of the challenge is that we're all different: My perspective on virtues may be different from yours, and we might get different utility from the same experience. And if I want to view my life as a work of art, that work of art is likely to be very different from the work of art that is your life. While there is great power in knowing more about what a "good life" means, in general, we are each most interested in our own individual good life. You know you can't conform your life to someone else's example and expect it to be "yours"—meaning a life that you can see as something that you crafted, that you made, and that feels like your life (rather than mine or someone else's). You don't want to pursue a good life that's generic or prefabricated—that wouldn't feel authentic or true to yourself. We each want to author our own unique version of the good life, to tell a story that only we can tell.

And yet we also want our lives to be more than our own little private creations. We want to share them with others, so that they see and appreciate the lives we've led and regard them as an example worthy of emulation. Even when we create a plan for a good life that fits our own unique selves, we draw on the shared fictions that make that life recognizably good to other people. We'd like others to see us as living a good life so that we can evaluate our choices by relying on something more than our merely internal sense of them—and so that we can help others by our example. For Aristotle, having that respect and appreciation from others made living virtuously much richer and more of an accomplishment. And it's true for most of us that part of the enjoyment of being virtuous is having the admiration and respect of our peers and community. We are social creatures, and we arrive at our convictions only as part of a community, relying on the shared fictions that unite us. The project is difficult, even paradoxical: We live for ourselves and for others at the same time.

MOVING FROM THE CLOUDS TO THE WORKSHOP: MAKING YOUR GOOD LIFE

I share these different perspectives on the good life to highlight some possibilities and provide some raw material for you to use as you work on a vision of your good life and then make plans for living it out. There is a lot here to help you. My intent is not that you get lost in the philosophical thicket and (sometimes) conflicting insights of these ideas. This discussion is meant not only to come back to you (so you can ask, How do these ideas lead me to see my life differently?), but also to be grounded in your experiences and sense of yourself. Any ideas about living a good life need to "fit" you, to resonate in your body and your mind, to be yours in a way that draws you to that life.

With that in mind, then, take a moment to step back.

Where are you right now? What do you hear, smell, see, and touch?

It's easy to forget to notice the present moment. We are rarely "here." We spend much of our time stressing about the future or replaying what happened in the past. While some of that "time travel" is necessary and part of being human, finding the time and space to be grounded—to be in the present moment and experience it fully—is also fundamental to living well. Each of the perspectives on the good life notes the importance of doing things that are good, yet an unappreciated part of the good life is enjoying that life: savoring what it is to be human and appreciating the richness and joy of your experiences. Far too many of us get caught up in "doing" and don't soak up the process of the doing or the gratification of working with others to make the world better (even in a relatively small way).

This also often plays out in the implicit attitude most people have about life. Without consciously thinking about it, we assume we will live forever, so we put off doing the things that might help us live more authentically, more fully in the moment, more happily. Although we will all die, and people who are close to death have unique and valuable perspectives on their lives, we struggle to see life as finite or to imagine the perspective of our older selves to help us think about our choices now. Of course, we can't really experience being near death until we get there. Yet, through empathy and listening to people who are confronting their own mortality, it is possible to gain significant insight into how we think about our current circumstances. In my "Ultimate Questions" course, one of the readings that is most impactful for students is a brief essay by a hospice nurse—someone whose job it is to work with people who are dying and to guide them on their final journey of this life—entitled "The Top 5 Regrets of the Dying."[8] The five most often-cited regrets are

1. "I wish I'd had the courage to live a life true to myself, not the life others expected of me."
2. "I wish I hadn't worked so hard."
3. "I wish I'd had the courage to express my feelings."
4. "I wish I had stayed in touch with my friends."
5. "I wish that I had let myself be happier."

Chances are, there is wisdom here for each of us in thinking about our own lives—as well as hints of some of the ways we are steering ourselves away from the life we really want to live, our own good life. But I share this list not to say "These are the five things you should focus on—only these," but to remind you that if you want to live a good life (however you see it), you need to take the time and effort to see your life as finite, to look at it from the standpoint of your final chapter, to truly imagine leaving this world, and then reflect on how you want to live now and all the days until you die. This is part of the power of one of the most beloved movies of all time, *It's a Wonderful Life*. While it may be a tad too sentimental for many, I find the film deeply affecting because it is a beautiful example of stepping outside our everyday perspective and truly trying to see our life anew—from the vantage point of our deathbed, or by imagining our world as if we hadn't lived at all.

A recent book, Matt Haig's *The Midnight Library*, offers another version of this thought experiment in a provocative and accessible way: From a very large library, the main character is allowed to check out different books—each of which, it turns out, represents a different life the character might have lived. This inspires the reader to sympathetically think about how their life might have gone had they made different choices, pursued different dreams, handled relationships differently. So many of us think about our lives as predestined—we were always going to do what we have done and our life was just going to work out this way. Haig pushes us to see how fragile and contingent our lives are. But for this choice, that conversation, this relationship—or, more generally, letting our fears and anxieties drive our decisions—we might have lived a very different life. While such thinking can be used to invite second-guessing and resentment, the spirit of the book is to encourage us to imagine what is possible. Who we might become. What story we want to write.

So how do we best imagine what is possible? How do we make, in the most effective and authentic way, the decisions that may prove consequential in our progress toward (or away from) our good life?

Design thinking is a tool used by many organizations not just to think about what they might do differently, but to do so in ways that are smart, relatively inexpensive, and fast, and that allow for both failure and learning, so that they can get closer to a true solution or direction. Rather than having to choose once and for all between two very different futures (e.g., building a giant new plant that eats up a huge portion of a firm's resources or finding ways to build new capacity in existing plants that are far less expensive but may not create enough change), design thinking provides techniques not just to imagine those two possibilities but also to actively envision both as realities, then gather information and feedback from key stakeholders to identify key challenges, come up with additions to the design to satisfy groups affected by it, and recognize potentially major hurdles that aren't visible without a "small-scale" experiment. Once a team has done a thorough job of vetting its ideas internally, the next step is to conduct a small-scale experiment with stakeholders to see if the assumptions are on target or need revision.

Design thinking offers a way of stepping into the imagined future (e.g., building a new product or plant) that allows a company to stress test many of the assumptions that need to be true for this new initiative to work while spending a small fraction of the resources that the full initiative would require. Starting small allows a team to "fail fast" and not waste tons of resources doing so if its plan is not sound. It can also provide important data to help company leaders see just how well their hopes for the initiative line up with the likely responses from stakeholders, allowing those leaders to make a better and more informed choice. This is not just a tool for companies. It is an approach we can all use. Many of my students do internships, spending a few months working for a company and an industry that gives them a window into a possible future. While this never answers all their questions and only sometimes clarifies their choice about which job to take, the ability to imagine and experience that future (even as a brief and limited experience) is a powerful tool that enhances their ability to make good choices that serve them. You can do this in your own life; experimenting and really trying out alternatives can help you go from a vague idea of the good life (perhaps just an abstract philosophical idea, or something only available to characters in movies) to shaping and developing a good life that is yours.

Another useful perspective on decision-making is courtesy of my colleague Saras Sarasvathy. According to her effectuation theory, entrepreneurs tend not to predict or plan the future, but instead to figure it out along the way, focusing on relationships and aligning with people whose passions are similar, experimenting, and taking feedback into account. As they meet each new potential stakeholder, they consider the question "What can we do?" This openness can lead to new possibilities, new resources, new commitments, new goals, new constraints, or new relationships (or none of those).[9]

While there are psychological roadblocks (like difficulty making decisions or being in the moment), there are also practical obstacles that can get in the way of the good life. It might be more or less challenging to live a good life depending on where and when we live, or whether we face special hurdles that limit our power to shape our choices (e.g., do we have certain basic rights to make decisions about our bodies and our lives—or not?). Achieving the good life might require some luck. Sometimes things outside our control—injury, abuse, illness, and so on—have a big impact on our ability to experience our lives as truly good. According to both Aristotle and Mill, we might face too much adversity or tragedy to see our lives as "good" in any meaningful way. Yet, as Frankl notes, some people can still make meaning of their lives in such difficult circumstances.

Sometimes we chase the wrong things or prioritize one thing so much that we lose sight of other aspects of life we need to really flourish. Researcher Brad Wilcox found that 75 percent of people aged eighteen to forty said that a career with a good salary was "crucial to fulfillment in life," compared to 32 percent who said marriage was; meanwhile, economist Sam Peltzman found that married people were 30 percentage points happier than unmarried people.[10] This does not mean, of course, that marriage is the answer; but it does suggest that prioritizing money and career over relationships might not create the happiness we envision.

Many people say money is a critical piece of living the good life, but few say they've found the good life by earning enough of it. In fact, having money sometimes seems to fuel the desire for more money rather than quenching it (as Aristotle warns). Some of the most money-hungry people on the planet already have more money than anyone else! And more money does not necessarily translate to happiness: Martin Seligman found that even in a period of fifty years when the gross domestic product of the United States tripled, overall life satisfaction didn't change.[11] We also know from the examples of many of the richest people that despite having more money than they could ever spend, they live their lives as though making more of it is the most important thing, preventing them from focusing on other things we see as integral to the good life.

Money is a fiction. It has value only because we decide it does. But money can get us many things that we do truly value. It can create a (limited) sense of security, provide us with food and shelter, enable us to support those who depend on us, and give us the structure and predictability that enable us to commit to our family and our hobbies. Our salary can bolster our pride in our accomplishments by helping us to build a sense of our worth. Having money makes space for experiences of value. Money is one of the trickiest elements to resolve as we plan and execute the good life. Most of us need a significant amount of it to live our good life. But many of us give up other aspects of the good life for its sake and may confuse a large bank account with evidence that we are living well. We often assume we need far more money than we really do—in part because we operate from a perspective that puts too much focus on money and not enough on the things that we truly value as part of our good life (time with friends and family, building new relationships or hobbies, self-care, doing activities we truly love, and so on).

For many of us, though, work (which, of course, is how most of us get money) plays a significant role in the good life. Of the five elements of Seligman's well-being framework, achievement can easily overtake the others—perhaps as a result of cultural conditioning. In the previous chapter, I touched on some of the pitfalls of relying too heavily on work to create a sense of purpose—your employer might exploit you and pay you less because you believe in its mission; you might spend so much time at work that you miss out on family and friends; your company might be lying about its mission, taking advantage of your work in a different, even more insidious way.

Working in a job that you value can give you experiences that you cherish. The daily practice of performing a labor of love can enrich your life, especially if that labor enables you to create things or enact change that you find meaningful. When we feel like we're creating enduring value by doing things we enjoy (or in which we find flow, or in which we can nurture our skills, or—ideally—all three), it not only gives us a sense of purpose; it makes our lives better. The problem is that sometimes work leads us to focus on goals that may not have enduring value for us, goals like making more money for our company or earning a more impressive title. And these goals can distract from other aspects of life that help us thrive. Work can get in the way of the good life even if we enjoy our jobs. At the end of the day, we're (usually) working for someone else, which can limit our choices. Focusing on jobs can cause us to lose sight of the possibility that we can have a good life quite apart from a job. As we get closer to a possible future where AI and smart machines "free" us from having to work, it may be essential for us to find things other than work to make up our good life.

But in the present, for those of us who do spend significant time at work, how can we find fulfillment in that aspect of our lives without making it our sole focus? How can we make sure our jobs contribute to our overall good life, while also prioritizing the other aspects, however we define them, of our good life?

Clayton Christensen's concept of the "marginal cost mistake" helps frame ways in which our desire to excel at work can systematically lead us to prioritize work and devalue our relationships with family and friends.[12] Imagine that, one evening, you are faced with a decision: to go home as you usually do to have dinner with your family, or to stay at the office a bit longer and make progress on an important report. You likely don't consciously decide that your work is more important than family, yet in the moment, faced with how to spend that time, it is much easier to choose work—to make one little exception, just this once, since the marginal cost of one evening in the office seems low. Over time, these situations can pile up, and you may find that you have come to overinvest your time and focus in work—even without consciously choosing to do so. It is easy to prioritize more time at the office and discount time with family and friends unless we notice this tendency and actively take steps to prevent it from distorting our priorities and undermining key aspects of our good life.

Another aspect of living a good life is what we do to help others try to live theirs. There is much about living a good life that is about us and our choices, yet so much of the writing on the topic presupposes that this good life is tied to being with others: partner, family, friends, community. We need to appreciate our own ideas for the good life in that context—what our vision asks of others and ways we might be making it harder for them to live their good lives. If we have a desire and a right to try to live our own good life, we should want to help others do the same. Indeed, utilitarian philosopher Peter Singer has argued that those of us who are affluent have a moral obligation to share our resources with people in poorer countries, to reduce their suffering and create conditions where it is more likely they can live a good life—something he terms *effective altruism*. He has also advocated for animal rights, to reduce animal suffering and to encourage more sustainable ways of eating (and living). Singer's work reminds us that part of our good life involves caring for others and doing what we can to help them live better lives—and recognizing some of the ways in which our trying to live our good life may impose costs and hardships on others that may be unjustified.

One other important dimension to note is the way in which giving to others and helping them (especially those less fortunate or living in hardship) can be an integral part of living your good life. As paradoxical as it may seem to some (though not to Aristotle, with his paradox about seeking happiness), numerous studies have shown that when we give to others and make their lives better, we tend to experience a boost to our own sense of happiness and positive feeling. This also makes intuitive sense. If we are social creatures and want to get along well with others, then we should take an interest in their well-being, including by doing things to make their lives better. This version of the idea is less about a moral duty or requirement to care for others and more about seeing ourselves as linked to others and doing things to help them out.

We can also see this focus on helping others show up in how we approach leadership and the good life. Many of our current conceptions of leadership focus on power and ego, drawing attention to the accomplishments of the leader (who often claims much of the credit for what their followers do). Yet other leadership models exist, ones in which leaders are grounded in helping others, serving something larger than themselves, and fostering an environment where people feel connected to each other and the mission of the organization. Even in relatively small acts, leaders can make a difference each day if they come to work with a mindset of doing so and serving others—an idea found in the concept of servant leadership.[13]

As Adam Grant shows, being a "giver" (rather than a "taker") not only feels good; it also makes you more desirable as a colleague and a boss—which benefits everyone.[14] Making a difference at work can simply involve taking time to talk to your employees and colleagues, making sure they know you are "for them," not just because you say so but because you show it every day in how you talk and act. It can mean making sure that you have a team of people who work well together, sacrifice some of their own interests for the good of the group, and share in the outcomes of their good work. People want to work for a boss who is for them. And it is much easier to be the kind of boss others want to have when you have had a boss like this, one who invested in you, saw your value, and treated you well even before you became a "star" at your job—so this kind of leadership is self-perpetuating and can improve a whole culture at work. While winning matters and makes life easier for everyone, how we get there and how we treat others matters even more, both for our own good life and in the service of creating sustainable results. When you treat people like humans (rather than cogs in a machine), invest in them, tell them the truth, and respect them (even when you may have to make hard choices), you build a team that also does these things. And a team that does these things well often outperforms a team made up of "stars" who lack the ability to work well together, to cooperate, and to allow others to shine.

In Grant's research, Seligman's well-being framework, Aristotle's ideas about eudaemonia, Frankl's search for meaning, and Bentham and Mill's ideas about utility, relationships are central to a good life. Many studies have demonstrated that the best way to be happy is to pour our energies into cultivating relationships, and to show up for others out of our desire to be "for them" and their success rather than because we expect a reward.[15] We all want a boss who cares about us and invests in our growth and development. Doing the same for others not only leads people to want to work for you, but it often makes for some of the most meaningful and enjoyable parts of work: truly making a difference in the lives of others. These findings support the idea that the good life for each of us is intertwined with the good lives of others; that helping others achieve theirs, even in relatively small ways that don't involve lots of time or resources, can make all the difference for you and for them. Rather than being a zero-sum game, the good life is something that can be expanded, shared, and cultivated together.

STUDENT VOICES

Having considered a few reflections on what might make for a good life—pleasure, relationships, meaning or purpose, accomplishments, and more—let's hear again from Robert, Joshua, Liniksha, Adanna, and Peter. Much of what drew them to my class was the prospect of discussing this question, and they continue to keep it in mind and develop their answers to it after graduating.

ROBERT

As we've learned, Robert sees himself as ambitious, helpful to others, and the product of random twists and turns of fate. He characterizes his life as "such a weird journey . . . I think it's all been logical, I think it's all been connected. But if one or two of the Ping-Pong balls had bounced in a different direction, it would have happened very, very differently for me." This of course is true for all of us: No one's life turns out as planned. But Robert seems to be particularly open to those turns and particularly willing to respond to them. His curiosity, he believes, has been a "driving force" in his life.

He also sees his good life as one full of relationship and connection.

When he imagines his own obituary, he worries about being alone: "I'm always cognizant of what people are going to say about me in the future. When I pass away, what is my lasting legacy and memory going to be? My favorite movie is *Casablanca*. My greatest fear was always, I'm going to be alone drinking at a bar, playing a game of chess by myself, like the character in *Casablanca*. I connected and related to him immediately as a teenager the first time I saw that movie, and I've seen it over a hundred times, for sure. I used to read *The Great Gatsby* every single year. And the main takeaway for me is, I don't ever want to be alone . . . and nobody should. Everybody loves this guy in life, except when he dies, he's all by himself, he's alone. And so this image has always resonated with me. I want to have a meaningful lasting impact on as many people as possible, for good purposes."

And connections have helped him throughout his life, from the judge who chose not to put him in juvenile detention to the prisoners he taught to play chess, and to his brother, whom he eclipsed in his twenties but never stops thinking about.

JOSHUA

Growing up, Joshua saw basketball as the "great equalizer"—the court was a place where he could connect with Black friends who weren't from his largely white neighborhood as well as non-Black friends from both neighborhoods. And based on his joy in the game and the tangible success of the professional basketball players he saw on TV, he decided that was the path to the good life. He recalls, "Growing up, we all thought . . . we have to make the NBA, and if I don't make it, we're not going to have the good life." Now, as an adult, his idea of the good life has expanded: "We can make an impact beyond just basketball. We can go to school. We can go to college. We can be in corporate America. We have opportunities and pathways there for us."

This breadth of opportunities that is part of his vision of the good life is made possible by and includes community: "Coming to the metropolitan region, just seeing the various cyber professionals—from testers to managers in upper positions, positions that I didn't see a lot of us in, in more southern areas—and then also, a network of the people I went to school with, seeing them embody that professionalism, and being able to be both. . . . Having so much culture, but at the same time being able to be cutting-edge researchers, developers, engineers: That showed me that I can be both."

His good life involves self-actualization, authentic connection, and building each other up: "appreciation and acceptance of everybody, belief in yourself, knowing that you can overcome, knowing that you can do all the things that you put your mind to."

LINIKSHA

When she considers what a good life means, Liniksha focuses on choices. While she embraces contradictory aspects of herself (victim, survivor, perpetrator . . .), she also sees her life as a series of choices and circumstances that invite more choices. "People are not their circumstances," she's decided. "People saw me as a victim [of child abuse], and in that time, I was a victim. But being a victim is not an identity. Circumstances are external things. They change. I also became the youngest graduate [in my MBA class]. That is a successful person, right? But then a year later, I got laid off. That's once again almost completely outside my control. . . . The things that were within my control were my choices." And she prides herself on those choices, that agency: "If you are present in making those choices, your gut, your heart, your intuition know what's the right one and what's the wrong one. Sometimes you have to make hard choices. I get that. But instead of deluding yourself and convincing yourself that's what the right choice is, which I think was oftentimes what my mom did, I want to be a person who looks at my options and then chooses the best choice that I can, given those options."

The ability to choose is central: "[In] death, you have no choice, and in life, you do. And so, if that is what we have in being alive, then I want to experience being alive fully. We're alive for a blip of a second and all we have in that lifetime is our choices. I'm not saying, 'Choose this,' or 'Choose that.' I'm not the ultimate decider of what's good [or] what's bad. But whatever your heart is telling you, if you're continuing to do that, I think that's a good life. [Those points] where I couldn't make my choices for me, or I felt like I couldn't make my choices for me: Those are the moments when I didn't want to be alive."

So, for Liniksha, a good life is defined by her ability to choose—with authenticity, honesty, and intention. "What's a good life?" she asks herself. "A life where you make choices for yourself. And sometimes if your hands are tied, maybe the only choice you can make is the breath that you're taking. But choose that breath. . . . And if you continue to make choices for yourself, that's a good life."

ADANNA

Adanna, too, realized the importance of choices—as we saw in the last chapter, her decision to quit her investment-banking job was the first time she'd chosen something for herself rather than continuing on the "hamster wheel." But she's learned that decisions, even those she makes authentically and honestly and with curiosity, can have effects she didn't intend, but ones she still learns from in her journey toward a good life.

She describes herself as very much an extrovert (and, as we learned in chapter 1, is often praised for her outgoing and kind personality) and "community driven." She grew up in a very large family—her father was one of thirteen children, and her extended family has "made it such a big deal to stay close. . . . My cousins are my friends. I do everything with them, go on holidays with them, talk to them every single day." And she went to a close-knit boarding school, "with the same group of people throughout, so I and my friends who went to that school are super, super close." And "in my boarding school, I was a prefect. I'm very big on my community and planning stuff." But she got burned out: "I don't know if it was the pandemic, but it got very, very exhausting, so I stopped doing it. But I felt like once I stopped, I stopped seeing people, and I stopped doing fun things. I [realized] I didn't want that to stop." In the process of experimenting with something new—solitude—Adanna realized how much community was a part of her good life.

Still, while she prioritizes community, the decision to step back from it, along with her observations of other important people in her life and her assessment of her own limits, led her to understand that boundaries are also important to her ability to flourish. She explains, "A lack of boundaries . . . is probably where a lot of my exhaustion came from. [I was] the go-to person, and always having all these expectations and always doing those things, because I cared. And I think about my cousins: I doubt I love my family any more than they do, but if they don't want to go somewhere, they don't go. Sometimes I'd be annoyed, but I [had to ask myself,] am I annoyed because they didn't show up? Or am I annoyed because I showed up and I felt I had to?" She is learning to check in with herself to see when she needs to set boundaries, when she needs to say no: "I have to start having those conversations with myself. I need to learn to start putting myself first, or resentment will start to build. That was happening because if I felt like I put a lot of effort in, and it wasn't reciprocated, I would start to feel resentful, even though no one asked me to do these things."

This process of figuring out what her good life is was thrown into sharp relief when several of Adanna's friends passed away in quick succession. She recalls, "There was a four-year stretch where at least once a year, someone I knew quite well passed away. I know that that drives a lot of the decisions I make. So I think it's one of the reasons why I just try to really live in the moment." And for Adanna, living in the moment means living in community: "Talk to everyone and reach out to everyone, because I never want to regret [not doing that]. I've always wanted to live life in a way that if someone calls me today and says, 'This person's passed away,' will I have regrets? And while it's a good thing, it's one of the reasons why I didn't have boundaries and I got very exhausted."

PETER

Peter, too, defines his good life partly through relationships, but much more with friends than with family: "I always got more [emotional support] from my friends, because I shared more of those passions so I could have more meaningful experiences with them. I was never close to cousins. I didn't grow up with them. So I stick with the people who are most meaningful to me, which end up . . . being all peers. I'm very happy with how my life has turned out. I love the relationships that I've had. I'm still working on building [relationships] with my family."

Peter prioritizes friends partly because, as he explains, he can share his passions with them and they can share theirs with him. He loves "analyzing something with someone I love."

And this focus on passions extends to other areas of his life, both work and play, so that he really defines his good life by his ability to pursue those interests: "I want the freedom to explore my passions, while also understanding that a career is important—maintaining a career that also ignites those passions in a way that's meaningful to me. I don't want my job to be all of my existence, and that's why I love the position I'm in right now. I really enjoy my job. It stretches me creatively. It works me really hard. But at the end of the day, I can still get off at a reasonable time. I can go watch movies. I can watch sports. I can spend time with my fiancée. I can cook. I can do all these things that I find really meaningful. Being able to explore these different avenues of my passions, I think, is the best life that I could ask for."

Passion, for Peter, has a meaning that extends beyond interest to also include a sense of rushing forward: "[The] good life for me is continuous advancement, always looking to continue to step up and step up and step up. I don't want to ever get to a point in my life where I stall, or I stay in one position or place, for a very long period of time. I think that would be, for me, not a very good life. I always want to be striving for the next [thing]. If it's a promotion, or just something new to do in my life, or moving upwards in my standing or monetary ability. I never want to take a step backward. I feel like if I ever took a step backward, then I would be falling."

Each of these people defines their good life in their own way, but they all continue to keep it in mind, to consciously consider what is part of their good life, how they can work toward that, and what might derail their progress. They are all, in their own ways, aware that their understanding and definitions of a good life have and will continue to change, as they find themselves in new situations and make new choices.

WORKSHOP ACTIVITIES

ACTIVITY 1: **Generate your four sentences on "What is the good life?"**

- What images, stories, or people come to mind when you think about how to live a good life?

ACTIVITY 2: **Generate your four sentences on "What is my good life?"**

- What about your good life?
- What things do you associate with a good life? Is it about a moment in time or a way of living?

- Are there things like money, fame, or external goods that are integral to your view? Why or why not?
- Take time to write your own view of yourself enjoying this life you have envisioned. Is this something you can truly see yourself doing?
- What do your friends and loved ones say? What might you be missing that they see about you and think would create sustained happiness for you?

ACTIVITY 3: Write your own obituary

- Take time to write a short obituary—something you could read out to others in sixty seconds or less. What do you want to be true about you and how you lived life? Try to avoid clichés and turns of phrase that you hear in most obituaries and focus more on the things that matter to you and that highlight a life that fits who you are (look back at your answer to the first ultimate question).
- Now that you know this, what does it mean in terms of what you should prioritize now? In the next five years? In the next ten years? What are some common pitfalls or mistakes you need to avoid (e.g., the marginal cost mistake, caring too much about money and not enough about experiences or relationships, or remembering that life doesn't go on forever)?

ACTIVITY 4: Design thinking

Try design thinking in your own life. As you contemplate a decision, instead of sitting back and agonizing, experiment. Get up, gather information, and explore not just what life might be like in those potential realities, but whether you'd enjoy it and whether stakeholders (family members, friends, colleagues) would support it and want to come along for the journey. Try out new activities, jobs, neighborhoods, and so on, so that you can make the choices that allow you to get closer to your good life and avoid the big mistakes that can be so devastating. If you take the time to really try to make an "alternative life" real, you might make a different choice than if you'd never fully considered it, let alone experienced it. Check out Bill Burnett and Dave Evans's *Designing Your Life* (in appendix 2) and try some of the exercises there.

ACTIVITY 5: The "why" exercise, again

Turn back to activity 3 in the last chapter and find the list of your core values. Consider how you can incorporate and live out those values in various parts of your life, and reflect on the things that tend to get in the way. What can you do to remove some of these barriers so that you can stay more connected to your values and shape how you approach work, life, friendship, and so on? Simply being mindful of these ideas and more intentional about framing what you do (and how you do it) can make a big difference in tightening the connections between the life you lead and the core values you espouse.

ACTIVITY 6: Finding a work-life balance

Jessica DeGroot[16] of ThirdPath Institute identifies some strategies to achieve a balance between work and nonwork activities that works for you:

- Be intentional about vacation, by doing things like scheduling trips for a time when work is less pressing, avoiding meetings on the days before and after a trip, and winding down or delegating projects before leaving.
- Be intentional about work, too, by scheduling time specifically for focused tasks without the distractions of email or similar interruptions.
- If you are a leader in the workplace, model a healthy work-life balance, to empower employees to do the same in whatever way works for them.

Clayton Christensen[17] offers "resource allocation" as another framing in which to consider work-life balance:

- If purpose happens outside of work, then make sure you limit your time at work so you can devote enough time to other things that matter to you.
- Alternatively, try to find ways to integrate your purpose into areas where it may not seem like a clear fit. For instance, you may see yourself as passionate about volunteer work and doing things to help others. While this seems like an after-hours kind of activity, chances are it is something you can incorporate into your work life too. Even if work is for profit, most companies value people who want to help cultivate human development and leadership at work.

ACTIVITY 7: **Put together a personal board of advisers**

This is a "hack" that both helps you find your good life and counters your blind spots and biases. Cobble together a small group of trusted friends and colleagues—people whose company you enjoy and who will speak the truth to you, even when that hurts. It helps to have some diversity in the group, at least when it comes to perspective and outlook on the world. Aristotle reminds us why having such a group is important: First, humans are really bad at seeing ourselves as we are—we tend to see ourselves as more heroic and virtuous than the rest of the world does. We need friends to help us see ourselves as others do so we can know ourselves better, not just to humble ourselves, but to see where we are truly virtuous and where we still need to learn, grow, and change. And second, we need friends to enjoy life, to share stories and experiences, to celebrate joys, and to offer support in moments of difficulty. Friendship is a critical part of the good life.

- Make sure you have a strong group of at least three people (and less than eight, just to keep it manageable and tight). Try to meet every few months, and be sure to mix catching up and having fun with talk about your life, relationships, goals, dreams, and fears.

- Don't look for answers or for the people in your group to fix your problems; do look for their honest feedback about how you see your situation, what the problem really is, and how you might think about it differently. Your advisers are not your fixers; they are the mirror you need to see things more clearly—while still making you accountable for your own life and choices. They can provide insight and support, even when that sometimes needs to come via hard truths that you have resisted or simply haven't seen.

ACTIVITY 8: Cultivate focus, courage, and curiosity

Penny Locaso[18] identifies lack of focus, courage, and curiosity as three reasons people gave for not living out their own good lives. She offers ways to build those skills, so that you can move toward yours:

- "Cultivating focus," she writes, "is about learning how to step away from the constant white noise of busyness. It's about creating the space to be, to think clearly, and to determine what truly matters to us so that we can include more of those things in our lives." To build this skill, delete the word "busy" so that you can describe your activities with intentionality (and also learn to say no).
- To cultivate courage, "lean into possibility" and stop using fear as an excuse to avoid something. Start small with acts of "micro bravery" like speaking up at a meeting.
- And to build curiosity, make a list of things you wonder about and set aside a few minutes each day to learn about them. To be more curious in your daily life, make slight shifts "to be fully present, to listen more than we speak, to ask more questions, be observant of new ideas, and embrace the unfamiliar."

CHAPTER 4

HOW SHOULD I GET ALONG WITH OTHERS?

Do to others as you would have them do to you.
—Luke 6:31

Everyone you meet is fighting a battle you know nothing about. Be kind. Always.
—Commonly attributed to **ROBIN WILLIAMS**

It is so easy to break down and destroy.
The heroes are those who make peace and build.
—**NELSON MANDELA**

The last ultimate question in this book is different. The first three took on our nature as a species alongside our nature as individuals. They addressed the collective identity, purpose, and good life of humanity, in order to give each of us a starting point for thinking about the different ways to make sense of these ideas for our own lives. They started with the general and arrived at the specific. This chapter goes, in a sense, in the opposite direction: It is about how specific individuals make up the group and asks how to relate across difference in a way that is authentic to you while honoring others, so we can come together to live peacefully and create a good society.

As I touched on in the previous chapter, we need to recognize how our ideas about our own good lives impact others—does our good life rely on burdens imposed on faraway others we may never meet? Can we own our good life as not just good for us, but as something that helps others? Does our good life include actively helping others find and live their own good lives? It is easy to lose sight of this last question, but for this to be a fully human account of ultimate questions, we need to be accountable for our answers—for what they might mean for others who have the same right to live and try to cultivate their good lives as we do. Especially since human history is filled with violence, war, systemic poverty, inequality, slavery, and other forms of brutality, we need to think through the implications of our answers for our fellow citizens and all others. And, as we face unprecedented challenges—a growing population, widespread poverty, increasing inequality, climate change—it becomes even more important to think about the ways our own answers to ultimate questions may impose substantial costs on others.

The first three ultimate questions establish very important kinds of difference. Indeed, much of this book, so far, has focused on ways in which we are different from others so that we can craft an identity, a sense of purpose, and a vision of the good life that suits us. This last question asks us to step back from that work and think about how to navigate the difference that our answers to the first three questions created. Because this takes on the issue of otherness directly, the distinction between the general and the specific form of the question collapses. When I think about how I should get along with others, I'm also, automatically, thinking about how others should get along with me, and how we should all get along together. In answering this question for ourselves, then, we also come up with ideas that can (and should) work for everybody.

This question of how to get along is especially important for us now, as our ability to do such things as talk civilly to our fellow humans (especially those we see as "different" or "other") has declined and seems to be eroding further by the day. Some basic assumptions about the US democratic process—like free and fair elections, candidates who accept election results, the peaceful transfer of power, leaders who govern for all Americans (not just their voters), and our ability to see people of the opposing political party as part of a larger "us"—have come into question. In short, this moment seems especially ripe for taking time to understand why tensions are so high and what we might need to do differently.

Part of what makes this topic hard comes from how humans are wired. We identify deeply with groups of people like us, our in-group. We put a great deal of weight on whether we identify as similar to (or different from) others. Some scientists argue that this tendency is connected to our evolutionary wiring. Martin Seligman argues that the big human brain is "a relationship simulation machine, and it has been selected by evolution for exactly the function of designing and carrying out harmonious but effective human relationships."[1] Psychologist and anthropologist Michael Tomasello suggests that "imitation and conformity" within groups of early humans was reinforced by group competition, as our long-ago ancestors collaborated with and protected each other.[2] By establishing a "we," complete with culture, language, and institutions, these tendencies paved the way for shared and individual sacrifice for the sake of our loved ones, our friends, our comrades, and the greater good. But by establishing a "them," they also reinforced the idea of an enemy to be struggled against. Even very small children, Tomasello found, enforce arbitrary social norms (rules of pretend play), which are really what distinguish groups of people from each other. While potentially malleable, these instincts are part of our biological heritage.[3]

IDEAS OF OTHERNESS

First, then, how do we imagine others? At the farthest reaches of otherness are nonhuman others with whom we interact and who seem to have some significant similarities to us: nonhuman animals and AI.

We humans have tended to see ourselves as above nature, superior to animals in ways that allow us to do all kinds of things to them that we would never do to those we consider fellow humans (even atrocities like slavery and genocide and war are often justified by considering the victims less than human). We can domesticate nonhuman animals, make them our pets, and largely treat them however we want. Humans not only kill animals and use them for meat (and other products), but we also allow corporations to create what are widely characterized as horrific conditions for how they are maintained, killed, and processed.[4] And we tend to ignore the rapidly increasing extinctions driven by human-caused climate change.[5] All this is justified by the fact that animals aren't humans and don't deserve the same kinds of protection or status.

As always, there are important thinkers who challenge the prevailing wisdom of society. Philosopher Peter Singer draws on the ideas of Jeremy Bentham (discussed in chapter 3) to argue that our moral obligation to decrease suffering extends to animals, who demonstrably are capable of suffering.[6] In the legal domain, law journals like the *Journal of Animal Law* publish research into the legal rights of nonhuman animals, which is used in court cases and legislation. Scientists are finding signs of unexpected animal intelligence not only in our close relatives like chimpanzees but also, recently, in farm animals: A 2023 *Science* article shared findings that "pigs show signs of empathy, goats rival dogs in some tests of social intelligence, and . . . cows can be potty trained."[7] And octopuses have been called "the closest we will come to meeting an intelligent alien."[8] Even trees and plants, to move further away on the evolutionary scale, seem to interact with each other and other organisms in something that might be called communication.[9] In short, many of the prevailing assumptions about animals (and how they are different from humans) are coming into question.

Despite this growing evidence that humans are not so different from (or superior to) animals (in terms of language, intelligence, genetics, the capacity for collaboration and moral behavior, and other factors), we have made relatively small changes in how we treat them. We should be curious about why—as well as what it would take to change our minds. If tomorrow morning you saw your dog holding up *The Wall Street Journal* and talking to you about yields in the bond market, would you shift your view of what a dog is—and what you owe your dog as well as other (similar) dogs and animals?

We can play this scenario out as well with a related trend that is growing in importance and can't be ignored any longer: the status of AI. We might see AI as simply a tool to use as we please. The computers that run AI are just machines, circuits and wires, electrons moving in a particular way according to the intentions of the humans who created it. We think nothing of scrapping a particular computer or robot if we own it and doing so serves our purposes. However, as AI grows in its ability to do things that approximate "thinking" in human terms and gains other human qualities (like the ability to use language, the development of individual identities and personalities, and even the creation of relationships with humans), the question of what we owe AI emerges, as does this one: At what point is AI enough like humans to deserve increased status? Even if we agree that AI isn't "people" the way humans are, at what point would it become enough like us that we should treat it like we do other humans: extend it rights and include it in human society?[10]

Moving closer, when we think of "others," the groups that usually come to mind are more familiar: people whose beliefs we understand but don't share. A Catholic person might know how Protestant doctrine differs from theirs, even though they reject it. An economically conservative person probably understands what it means to distrust the free market, even though the free market is something they embrace. We might vehemently object to the customs, beliefs, and assumptions of these other groups, but together they form nodes on the coordinate plane in our minds on which our own group is located. As they individually confront us as adversaries, together they're also part of what gives our own group its distinctive shape. Because we are tribal and seek to be in groups that align with who we are, we unconsciously create all kinds of demarcations that generate new forms of otherness. In some sense we need others to know who and what we are. We just don't pay as much attention to the unintended implications of those choices, especially when we start to treat these others in ways we didn't intend.

Sometimes otherness is hard to see. Within groups, there might be elements of difference that aren't at first visible. When I first came to Darden, I met a new colleague, Paul, whom I came to admire. Soon, however, I discovered that he was a Florida Gators alumnus and fan. As a graduate of the University of Tennessee, I really dislike the Florida Gators, and I began to think of Paul less as an ally and more as a rival. An aspect of identity as trivial as a sports team allegiance genuinely colored my attitude toward a colleague! I'd like to think that the change in my attitude was jovial and good-natured, but in fact this new knowledge of Paul's allegiance touched on something deeply automatic and even primitive: a reflexive sorting instinct that caused me to briefly regard him as the enemy. That feeling didn't last beyond some friendly ribbing, but it goes to show that the divisions we make happen swiftly, they're colored by attitudes of approval or distrust, and it's difficult to predict which markers will matter and which won't.

Whether the otherness we're encountering is (figuratively speaking) close or far away, whether we encounter it in the form of a rival or an ally, whether it's obvious or hidden, it poses the question of how to relate. That's because otherness always comes paired with a kind of attitude. That attitude might be one of bewilderment and confusion, antipathy, grudging respect, appreciation, or even fear or love.

This attitude may feel automatic, but it's important that we notice it. We have to ask ourselves what otherness means to us, and how we're going to relate to other people. This question seems more relevant every day: As I write this book in 2024, I can see any number of fault lines in the world.

American politics provides an obvious example. In the United States, our ability to just "get along" seems to have suffered a rather rapid decline. As one small indicator of how things have gotten, this is the first time in my life when I can envision the United States having a second civil war—and in fact, a recent Hollywood movie that imagined a modern civil war grossed well over $100 million. We have had plenty of conflict and disagreement in my sixty years, yet none of that compares to what we are seeing now. Numerous indicators suggest we are struggling to get along with others in some fairly profound ways. According to 2024 Pew Research studies, a strong majority of Americans find it "stressful and frustrating" to discuss politics with people with opposing views, and a decreasing minority see any common ground at all between the two parties.[11] As part of my own teaching over the past few years, I've heard increasingly from students who are terrified to share their political beliefs for fear of ostracism and the loss of important relationships. The disappearance of bipartisanship in American politics, and with it the capacity to evaluate candidates based on their stances rather than their party affiliations, has shrunk our ability to have open but friendly conversations about our most deeply held political beliefs with people we don't already agree with—conversations that could otherwise lead to growth and mutual benefit, not to mention policy innovations that benefit all Americans. All too easily today, those conversations turn to anger, hatred, and even violence. My own campus has been touched by that violence. On August 11 and 12, 2017, marchers with the Unite the Right rally—avowing the supremacy of the white race and advocating for a political program that matched that belief—descended on the University of Virginia. Violence spread through downtown Charlottesville as onlookers were horrified by the growing conflict and open physical altercations in one of the most important parts of the city. By the time the protesters had left, Heather Heyer, a young woman from the Charlottesville community, had been killed, intentionally struck by a car driven by a young man who supported Unite the Right.

Religion, another source of division, has always been polarizing. It speaks to ultimate truths like the nature of reality and the moral obligations that these ultimate truths imply—often involving injunctions to persuade or force people to live in accordance with those obligations. Religion has been a source of incredible kindness and generosity toward other humans, but it has also been a powerful tool used to support unimaginable cruelty. World history is full of wars that either were about religious differences or were heavily influenced by religious elites from different religious groups; violence is even now, as I write this, being committed in the name of religion (e.g., in Gaza and across the Middle East). Whether causally or incidentally, religious differences are linked to animosity and violence among rival human groups. It seemed for a while that we had reached a more enlightened phase of our collective history, one where we could navigate religious differences amicably and even appreciate them for their own sake. That fragile modus vivendi appears to be weakening under the pressures of the modern world.

In what seems like anticipation of this challenging dynamic, most religions have directives in scripture or wisdom traditions that encourage believers to treat those outside their religion peacefully and with respect. Documents like the Ten Commandments don't say "just for Jews or Christians"—they are meant to apply to all. The parable of the Good Samaritan, in which a stranger from a different sect is the only one to help a traveler who has been horribly abused on the road, is quite explicit in saying that not only should you not persecute religious others, you should go out of your way to help them.[12] While most religious scriptures seem to justify violence against those of a different religion at certain points, at others they espouse tolerance and respect for those outside their faith community. Perhaps this tension is based in that very human "in-group, out-group" conundrum: We have evolved to cooperate and collaborate to an astonishing degree, but the flip side of that cooperation is the hyperawareness of those outside our group, those who do not cooperate, those who, consequently, we treat as less deserving, even less human.

Religious parables and laws enforcing tolerance and peace are paralleled in secular, civil society through shared norms and mechanisms intended to level the playing field, to limit this bias we have against others, and to create more just outcomes—as well as end the kinds of disputes that can otherwise drag on and blow up into larger social skirmishes that most groups prefer to avoid. Some countries, like the United States, have created not only laws protecting vulnerable groups but also shared assumptions that downplay our differences and elevate our shared identity as Americans over differences in where we come from, what languages we speak, and what cultures we identify with. Yet such norms can only do so much, especially in the current political moment, where such differences—between "immigrants" and "Americans," for example—are being elevated in both social and political conversation. As I write this in the closing weeks of 2024, it's clear that this talk is more than just random philosophizing about identity; it may well lead to mass deportations of people who consider themselves American and were previously free to remain in the country.

Thus, along with religion and political affiliation, nationality is an important fault line of difference and conflict. We're especially likely to notice differences between ourselves and other people when we travel abroad. Citizens of different countries speak different languages and have different customs. We often see these differences as neutrally curious, or enriching, or horizon expanding, but they also pose barriers to understanding and connection. And they can form the foundation for divisions between "us" and "them" that are adversarial and even violent. In the United States as in many nations in these early decades of the 2000s, immigration has become a particular political flash point. And while we might have flattered ourselves a few decades ago that the important sources of conflict between countries had been resolved and that wars between the most powerful nations were a thing of the past—that we'd reached the "end of history" (as an important book on the subject claimed)—that illusion too seems to have left us. We're now witnessing a renewal of the kinds of large-scale military campaigns that only recently we regarded as a relic of the past.[13]

Scores of other sources of otherness deserve attention: gender, race, culture, language, and sexual orientation, just to name a few. I encourage you to think deeply about these and how you approach them in your life.

Just as the human talent for collaboration also resulted in rivalries and wars, sources of otherness are also sources of identity, and in this way, aspects like political affiliation, religion, and nationality are intimately connected to our exploration of ultimate questions. These categories are often proxies for deeper beliefs about identity, purpose, and happiness. And so as we consider how to get along with others, we necessarily keep the forms of otherness that are based on differing answers to ultimate questions in the background.

I invite you now to consider that particular form of otherness that is the result of differing answers to ultimate questions—not the forms of the otherness (nationality and so on) that might be behind some of those differences, but the answers themselves. The lens of curiosity and questioning is a powerful one, because the beliefs we have about ultimate questions are both our most powerful and our most freely chosen. And we ought to be curious about why the moral norms, stories, and wisdom that help us get along with others seem to carry so little weight when it comes to how people actually behave. Turning the other cheek, stopping to help someone from a rival tribe who is injured and needs help, treating others with compassion: All of these sound like the kinds of things that might go a long way in helping us do a better job when it comes to interacting with people we see as other. But our history suggests that we tend to do the opposite—that too often we see others not only as different, but also as somehow not deserving of respect, decency, or compassion. Why, exactly, are these noble injunctions to treat others well doing such a poor job of shaping how we behave?

As it turns out, we have learned quite a bit about human psychology, at both the individual and group levels, that casts light on this question. In an influential and disturbing set of experiments, psychology researcher Stanley Milgram wanted to understand how humans would really treat others when they were placed in a challenging context.[14] Milgram was horrified by what he had seen in German concentration camps and wondered whether a similar thing could happen in the United States. He conducted a series of experiments to explore how much individuals would protect their fellow citizens in the face of requests from an authority figure to inflict harm on them.

In his studies, Milgram found that we are predisposed to follow authority and to mistreat those outside our group. In his study, an authority figure instructed participants to pull a lever to "shock" a "learner" (actually an actor; there was no actual electricity delivered) every time the learner couldn't recall the correct answer to a set of word pairs they were asked about. The shocks began at 15 volts and increased in 15-volt increments with each wrong answer. The highest possible shock level was 450 volts, and there were verbal indicators like "danger—severe shock" and "X X X" below the high numbers. The learner also made audible (and escalating) protests with each shock. Despite the learner asking to be let out of the experiment, complaining of a heart condition, refusing to answer any further questions, and finally ceasing to make any sound (around 330 volts), well over half the participants continued to shock all the way to the highest level. In short, they thought they were killing a perfect stranger who had done them no harm, solely because an authority figure had asked them to do so.

Milgram's experiment also sheds light on the power of proximity. The closer we get to the authority figure (in the experiment, they were in the same room), the more power they have over us, but as they move farther away (e.g., outside the room, across the country, accessible only by email), the less power they tend to have. A similar but opposite dynamic emerged regarding the victim—the person who was being shocked. As the participant dishing out the punishment got closer to the learner (e.g., in the same room), the participant tended to stop sooner—but as the distance between the participant and the learner increased (e.g., they were in separate rooms with a microphone, then in separate rooms with no microphone), it became easier for the participants to shock more. This finding fits with our everyday experience of life online (a fairly remote and removed kind of social interaction): We are far more willing to say and do things we would never consider if we were in the same room as another person, yet in the context of the internet, such behavior becomes normalized. Salience and psychological proximity matter and powerfully shape how we behave even when we aren't aware that this is going on.

In the Stanford Prison Experiment, often discussed in relation to Milgram's study, Philip Zimbardo (a close friend and colleague of Milgram's) recruited twenty-four young men to be either prison guards or prisoners in a mock prison he created in a dorm at Stanford University.[15] While the study was designed to last two full weeks, over the first three days, the guards grew steadily more abusive and authoritarian, while the prisoners grew first rebellious and then increasingly helpless, passive, and depressed. Audio reports and photos from the experiment show horrific levels of abuse by the guards against the prisoners. The experiment was ended after six days. It is another graphic illustration of how, when humans are in a context of power, we are capable of doing horrific things to perfectly innocent peers. Once we take on a given social role (in this case, a "guard" or a "prisoner"), we are not only able to do some awful things to others; we may even feel obliged to do so.

Milgram's and Zimbardo's experiments have been denounced for ethical and procedural lapses and could not be repeated today (they were done from 1960 to 1963 and in 1971, respectively—and protections for human subjects were later created to prevent studies like these from being replicated), but, along with historical events, they function as powerful cautionary tales about the extremes people may go to in order to follow orders from authority figures and to fulfill their given roles.[16] In short, they show that we can't count on others to treat us well. From the standpoint of these studies, the Good Samaritan who stops and helps a stranger in need is more the exception than the rule—and that, given certain conditions, it is perfectly possible for me to kill an innocent stranger for no reason at all.

But there are also signs of hope and clues about how groups can limit the power of authority, the primacy of group identity, and our unconscious tendency to treat others badly. As neuroscientist Leor Zmigrod points out, in these and similar experiments, "there was always a percentage of participants who resisted conformity or obedience.... There were consistent outliers to universal authoritarian tendencies."[17] Some people have an innate ability to resist authority and to question the framing given them by an authority figure. In the Milgram studies, the authority figure said the experiment was a scientific study on memory learning. There was much in the design of the study to reinforce that narrative. Yet there were several other competing narratives—like being asked to seriously harm a perfectly innocent stranger. In fact, over 40 percent of the participants had some doubts about whether the shocks were actually being administered. In the end, though, they "defaulted to truth," which is how Malcolm Gladwell describes the "operating assumption ... that the people we are dealing with are honest."[18]

Especially in the United States, we like to think we are independent, that we challenge and resist authority, that we live our values and stand up for what is right. These studies, along with countless stories from organizations of all stripes, support a far different reality: We mostly do what we are told, and we do so without the limits of conscience. While this reinforces a view that people behave more like sheep following a shepherd than independent choosers who do what they want, knowing this tendency allows us to approach life with others differently. As evolutionary biologist Richard Dawkins puts it in his seminal book, *The Selfish Gene*, "Let us try to *teach* generosity and altruism. . . . Let us understand what our own selfish genes are up to, because we may then at least have the chance to upset their designs, something that no other species has ever aspired to."[19] Because we're not simply bound by our evolutionary heritage to follow group norms, we can bring those norms under conscious reflection and consider whether those instincts make sense, whether they still serve us, and whether or when we want to heed them. It takes conscious awareness of these forces to reshape how things work in organizations. If we approach the task with intention and lots of practice, we can help people speak the truth to their bosses, share bad news, and resist the tendency to treat others as scapegoats. In short, bringing this fourth ultimate question to the foreground is vital to our ability to treat others better: to live out the true respect and decency we aspire to.

All this research provides a very different perspective on the challenge of getting along with others, especially since there are so many ways in which we see ourselves as different from others. We have different gender identities, nationalities, ages, and religions. We affiliate with different political parties, belong to different clubs, schools, or trivia teams. We identify as belonging to different races, or ethnic groups, or clans, or fiefdoms—"fictions" in the sense Yuval Noah Harari writes about: "None of these things exists outside the stories that people invent and tell one another."[20] These are differences we create to differentiate "us" from "them." And even when we are similar to each other in all the supposedly important categories, even including the same deeply held beliefs, we are still different because we each inhabit a separate consciousness and live in a unique body. I am not you and you are not me, even as we can empathetically try to see the world through each other's eyes. We struggle with how to get along, what we owe each other, and how we should treat each other.

APPROACHING OTHERNESS THROUGH ULTIMATE QUESTIONS

As we've explored throughout this book, our answers to ultimate questions connect us to something deep within our natures, but they are also answers we choose. My definitions of myself, my purpose, and my good life reflect my deepest understandings of how I fit in, and they express how I decide to stand out. The answers to ultimate questions reflect how, at the center of our human existence, we author ourselves. In this crucial way, they are distinct from other aspects of our nature, such as race or nationality, that are more or less given to us (even though these too can be things we shape, choose among, and allow to play small or large roles in our identity). The answers to ultimate questions are our creations.

That creative aspect of our answers also implies something special about how we relate to people with different answers. It connects us to those people in a way that's different from how we're connected across differences of race, nationality, or religion. Our ability to freely choose our answers, and to stand out from others by making those choices, depends on the existence of people who choose differently than we do. In a deep and direct way, we are linked to the people who answer ultimate questions differently, and our choices can be enriched by theirs (and vice versa). If we see all humans as equally morally worthy, then we are curious about their answers to ultimate questions and don't assume that difference is the same as conflict. We need to do the work of reflecting and discussing before we decide that such differences are too great for us to get along—and whether we will treat "them" differently.

This is partly because we define ourselves in relation, but also because conversations are a key part of the process of working through ultimate questions. We learn more about ourselves—our values, our purpose, our ideas of the good life—when we ask others about theirs, and when they ask us. We've all been in conversations when we realize, in the process of explaining something, that we don't fully understand it or haven't thought through all the implications. In talking with someone who doesn't have the exact same assumptions and understandings as we do (in other words, any other person), we develop ideas and help them develop theirs: We learn.

When we reflect on our own answers to ultimate questions, alone and in conversation, we gain a richer sense of our own nature, and we're confronted with a more vivid picture of how we're different from others. Ultimate questions establish a very important form of otherness. By talking about them with people who answer them differently, we gain a new perspective on others and new tools for relating to them. At the same time, it's important to note that nothing, including conversations about ultimate questions, can ensure that we can get along with everyone all the time. Indeed, given the kind of beings we appear to be, that kind of "happily ever after" take on getting along with others seems like an odd and ill-fitting aspiration. There are often good reasons to treat other people differently and occasionally to separate ourselves from them (think of a harmful intimate relationship, for example).

So what does approaching otherness through the lens of ultimate questions teach us about how to navigate it?

When we encounter otherness, we often see it as a kind of onerous moral challenge, a test of our ability to accept and appreciate people who are different from us—a test we often fail. And as the differences seem more and more intractable, this appears to be increasingly true. Answers to ultimate questions aren't like that. Two people can profoundly disagree about the nature of identity, purpose, and happiness, and still at some level understand each other's mindsets. Both are wrestling with the same questions, after all, and both are choosing their answers—often in a conversational process that relies on interpersonal differences. And because the questions are the same (one reason I've included philosophers and scientists in this book is simply to show that people have been working on these questions since humans first appeared on the earth), the process invites empathy. There's a deliberate thought process behind your choices that others can try to imagine, even when they disagree with your assumptions and conclusions. Our answers to ultimate questions are powerful precisely because they are choices, which means we could have chosen differently. The fact that other people come up with different answers doesn't detract from our answers—it enhances them. As Martin Buber writes, "Only as long as [a person] enters into the relation [with others] is he free and thus creative."[21] Other answers allow us to see our own more clearly—and they invite humility. None of us knows it all. Each of us makes assumptions about the world, including our answers to the four ultimate questions; and that humility can enable us to continue to see the humanity and moral worth of others—to keep us from going too far in what we do with such differences.

And we can apply this same empathetic, creative approach to other kinds of difference. Focusing on ultimate questions highlights the differences related to our deepest values and beliefs, which are in turn products of our most powerful and intimate choices. Strangely, that makes the challenge of difference more navigable, because it makes our differences amenable to understanding and discussion. What's more, it transforms our differences from sources of danger and liability to sources of deep value and understanding. When people are simply born different, it can be difficult to imagine their experiences. But when those differences are deliberate and chosen, they become imaginable, even when the conclusions this other person draws are very far from our own. And once we can imagine and welcome—even invite—those differences, it becomes much more possible to do the same with other kinds of difference.

In the realm of ultimate questions, we navigate getting along with others through conversations that are deep and vulnerable and even dangerous, but that enable us to see each other in all our complexity and to begin to understand how people think differently from us. How much more creative and fruitful could those conversations be if we opened them to other kinds of difference as well? In my "Ultimate Questions" class, I witnessed students experience some of the most powerful learning of their lives in honest and frank conversations with others whom they previously had seen as bad, wrong, or even evil. As I've mentioned, one requirement of the class involved small groups (designed intentionally to be heterogeneous) deciding on learning experiences that would invite wrestling with these questions, then actively taking part in the chosen activities, and finally sharing their reflections with the rest of the class. In one particularly memorable example, a Jewish student reached out to a Palestinian in Gaza to talk about the war there. In another, a group of students, several of whom believed that nonheterosexual orientations were sinful and deeply wrong, talked to the partner of a student in class about when he had come out as gay and taken a stand on behalf of other LGBTQ+ people in the military. Given the topics and the backgrounds of those involved, both of these conversations could easily have gone very badly, resulting in lots of conflict, hostility, and very little learning and empathy. Yet the people involved came away grateful for the experience, having learned important things about how they understand ultimate questions, and more willing to do this work in their own lives. Talking about these experiences and conflicts is not easy; they can bring up painful memories and lead to conversations that are hard, emotional, and vulnerable. (Please see the first section in appendix 2 for some resources on navigating difficult emotions.)

There is no question that getting along with others is a huge challenge for us as humans. There are many ways in which we operate as groupish and tribal creatures who can easily be led to horribly mistreat people outside our group: to depict them as less than human, scream insults and profanities, degrade and humiliate them, cause physical violence, and even see them as deserving to be killed. If we are going to make any progress in improving how we get along with others, we need to start by facing this hard truth. Human decency and conscience are no match for these impulses in human nature. If we want to craft a better future in how we get along, it needs to be grounded in these realities and supported by leaders and organizations who wield their power intentionally to work for peace and encourage mutual respect. It will take creativity, imagination, and bravery. This is another reason why we need to attend to ultimate questions and engage in the work they ask of us.

The ability to sit across from and have an open conversation with someone else can be one of the most valuable sources of insight about others and how we define that otherness—as well as one of the richest ways to connect with and know others. We all want to be known, to talk about things that matter to us, to learn about others and form rich relationships. One of the best ways to do all these things is to find ways to discuss ultimate questions with others, especially those who see the world differently from us. If we know the challenges of these kinds of conversations and have the tools to help keep the discussion from going sideways, we have a better chance to create positive interactions that produce understanding, respect, and collaboration (rather than reinforce differences, create disrespect, and undermine our ability to collaborate).

GETTING ALONG WITH OTHERS AT WORK

Of course, some are tasked with considering the question of how to get along with others in ways that affect many more people. They set policy for the rest of us, shape foreign relations, or dictate national domestic policy. Aristotle thought that the best expression of human virtue was not just an individual good life but a life in politics, the "master art," for the goal of "human good."[22] Bentham and the utilitarians, too, considered the community paramount; they are often described as social reformers, since they held that laws and actions are good only if they help and do not hurt people, and that the best laws are those that help the most people.[23]

The challenge for most of us is not quite so grand. As a private citizen, I can't influence larger entrenched relations to otherness. You're likely not in a position to dictate US immigration policy or to decide how the United States should engage with Russia. But you and I can decide how to navigate otherness in our own lives. And you might even be in a position to shape relationships within teams that you lead or are a part of. The question of how to get along with others isn't external to everyday existence. It's part and parcel of how we live within our families, communities, and professional organizations. It's something we navigate every day, from the moment we wake up to the moment we go to sleep. I encourage you to view this question as having practical implications in your day-to-day life.

This question is especially pertinent for those of us working in business and management. In a pre-class survey, I ask the students in my class whether they agree with the prompt "For me to be an effective leader I need to share some aspects of how I answer ultimate questions; and, for me to be an effective leader, I need to be able to learn about some aspects of how my followers answer ultimate questions." Students respond overwhelmingly in the affirmative. Most of my students view this kind of reciprocal sharing and vulnerability as an important part of leadership and teamwork, even (and especially) when it reveals differences within teams. They believe that leadership and teamwork require us to be authentic and honest about what we care about, in order to be fully seen and known. It's then up to the leaders and the members of the team to navigate these differences. Research backs up this intuition: When leaders focused on values that helped stakeholders, rather than only on profits, "employees were more likely to perceive transformational leadership . . . and therefore expend extra effort in their work, which predicted firm performance."[24]

Framing matters. We all tend to think along the lines of an existing framework. Recall that at the beginning of my "Ultimate Questions" class, I asked students to read several short pieces and also come up with four sentences that distilled their thoughts on "who we are." I never received a poem or an equation (arguably two of the most distilled ways to express an answer to this question), and most of the responses were related to the readings in some way. Leaders can use this quality—this very human tendency to think within established boundaries—for authoritarian purposes, sure, but they can also tap into it in more benevolent ways. Researchers have found that "when the prisoner's dilemma task is framed as relational by referring to it as 'the community game,' participants are more likely to cooperate and improve each other's outcomes. When the same task is framed as competitive by calling it 'the business game,' participants are more likely to focus on their self-interest, defect, and suffer worse outcomes."[25]

Otherness is especially salient in the arena of international business. When our business ventures cross national borders, we must decide how to deal with differences in customs around, for example, bribery and the treatment of women, or legal differences around worker protections and environmental standards. Sometimes those differences are profound, such as when we encounter a legal regime that fails to regulate or prevent the use of child and forced labor. We might on the one hand feel a need to adapt to local conditions and on the other feel like there are certain lines we won't cross. We might acknowledge the necessity of compromise in order to "get along," even when it comes to our values, while still recognizing that compromise and "getting along" have limits. These dilemmas grow in importance as the world becomes more interdependent and as the tensions caused by these differences intensify.[26] In such arenas as climate change, access to natural resources, business norms, and human rights, the issues raised by these dilemmas are of increasingly vital importance.

As humans, we're powerfully susceptible to the impulse to divide the world into "us" and "them," and then to regard "them" with animosity and distrust. We have reflexive, automatic answers to the question of how to get along with others. But, at the same time, "*other people* are the best antidote to the downs of life," writes Martin Seligman.[27] The process of working through ultimate questions—on our own, but especially in conversation with people with whom we disagree—can turn that otherness into something of value, something that encourages creativity and empathy.

STUDENT VOICES

Throughout this book, and especially in this chapter, the focus has been on conversation. But reading is essentially a solitary activity. Part of the reason I've included the stories and quotes from my five former students is to simulate a kind of conversation on the page—I hope that reading them offers you a glimpse of the kind of relationship across difference that discussing ultimate questions can invite.

ROBERT

Although many of Robert's choices seem to be in response to, or in competition with, his older brother, he loved and idolized him: "I still miss him every day." And throughout his many endeavors, from teaching to serving in the military and now working in the corporate world, Robert highlights connection with others. He recalls a change of heart around this: In his summer of reading, when he was grounded after being arrested for stealing, he "read every word ever written by Ayn Rand, and I used to think being an altruist is like a horrible, horrible thing." But, he learned, altruism "made me feel good. It made me feel good to get hugged by a person in jail who's going to get a paper to go to their parole board with because I taught him how to play chess. It made me feel good when I taught students fractions by shooting basketballs into a hoop."

And this good feeling, he realizes as he considers this fourth ultimate question, is also a source of personal growth, returning to the first question. In reflecting on his experiences teaching chess in prisons, he says, "It was altruistic, but also a larger sense of it's growing me as much as they [the incarcerated students] are growing from me."

JOSHUA

As we've seen, Joshua deeply values continuous learning and human connection. And while the process of working through ultimate questions has helped clarify those values for him, it took a moment of crisis to really change his perspective on how to live with different others.

In his mid-twenties, Joshua was admitted to the emergency room with an asthma attack so severe that he feared for his life. On his treatment team in the hospital was Jenny, a respiratory therapist who was his demographic opposite: a white, lesbian woman. He recalls his attitude before this experience: "By nature, I'm . . . all about community. But I was very closed off [and not] receptive to change. If I had seen Jenny in the store, I probably would not have stopped to talk to her." Unable to speak because of the asthma, Joshua wrote on a piece of paper, "Am I about to die?" And Jenny "kind of chuckled, but [said,] 'I can't answer that,' but what she did do was, [even though] I never knew her and never met her before then, she was like, 'I will sit here and hold your hand.'"

Joshua recalls the deep comfort of that simple gesture from a stranger: "I knew I was gonna die but I wanted to hold her hand. I never would have thought I'd be in the hospital, probably on my deathbed, holding a complete stranger's hand whose sexual orientation was antithetical . . . to Christian norms, and finding so much comfort and connection and appreciation for somebody to hold my hand."

This experience was a breakthrough for Joshua in his perceptions of others: "It broke the barrier for me" about "everything that I felt like I was conditioned to think about people, no matter [their] sex, creed, color, religion." He decided that "after that moment, I'm not about to live life in this box. I'm going to see the good in people, I'm going to try and find it, and if they want to show me that good, then we'll be a lock."

Joshua vows to live out the lesson he learned that day: "take it upon myself to truly be that catalyst to make sure that everybody can find positivity in life. . . . I want to make sure that I'm a giver, that I'm gifting something. I don't know if it's going to be time, [or] money, or conversations, but that acknowledgment of your humanity, and the value you may and you can bring, is very much what I want to give, very much what I want the world to be, and what I strive for. . . . I can make that connection with people."

And he wants not only to connect with and build up people, but also to seek out difference and learn from those others: "Let's travel. Let's see other cultures. Let's hang with people who are not like us, or who don't have the same type of background." He brings that back to business, and his teams: "I want to be this mosaic portrait of these individuals. How do they show up? What were their experiences? How have they been able to overcome? And then how do they continue to push forward, knowing that there may be blockers?"

LINIKSHA

As a child of abuse, Liniksha has struggled with what it means to get along with others. In leaving behind her family and beginning a new life in a new country, she had to cut ties with her mother completely. She turned inward after that break and now sees herself as the caregiver she never had in her parents: "It's a sense of having a control over myself that is friendly. I'm friends with myself."

And despite (or perhaps because of) her emphasis on the importance of choices in a good life, she makes those choices in a nurtured and nurturing way: "I'm not forcing myself or pushing myself. It's like every cell in my body, every fiber of my being, wants to do what's best for me."

When she was still living with her mother, and even after she left but before she successfully cut ties, she felt like she was still being controlled by her mother: "I guess that's . . . how you know that you are being captured by somebody and you're a hostage to somebody is when you listen to their voice in your head above your own." And her experience of immigrating from a country where she was seen as "less than" because she is a woman to one where the discrimination is (primarily) racial instead has taught her that these kinds of judgments are arbitrary, giving her the power to more fully define herself. Now, on her own, "I finally feel free." Today, Liniksha says, "What's driving me is my heart. I'm able to quiet all the voices in my head. There's just a united, singular soft voice inside of me, and that's what guides me."

So, she begins by fostering a healthy and loving relationship with herself. From there, she does the same with others: "How I get along with others is how I get along with myself. So, there's no distinction for me."

ADANNA

Adanna, too, learned about herself by stepping back from her large and close-knit community of friends and family—and while she discovered that she needs boundaries and some limits to her own eagerness to help, she also learned that she deeply needs her community. In that process of finding and building her own boundaries, Adanna felt that she also affected her friends and family: "That's one big thing that I guess I've been learning. [It is my friends and family] who suffered the most because they had enjoyed the most access to me, and then incorporating these boundaries . . . had to lead to some adjustments to the friendships." Much of that adjustment seems to be trusting herself, so that she, like Liniksha, can nurture her needs and take care of herself. It also means expecting of others what she expects of herself: "I need to know, when things get tough, who are the people that I absolutely need to be there for? Or can even help [me] to fill [my] cup to get better? Because some people just take and take, and those are the people that I can't really be around now. It doesn't mean I'm never going to be around them. But until I feel like I have something to give, I probably [won't be] around them. I think those are the things that I've learned in this period of solitude. As much as I'm an extrovert, and I get my energy from being out, . . . now it's just any kind of external environment I like being in. So, [I'm] trying to find the things like, 'Do I go . . . out dancing because I love music? Or do I want to be in a place where it's a safe space and we obviously talk about real life?'"

And as she learns to ask herself these questions, Adanna feels that she is living more authentically, which affects those around her: "I like the fact that if I respond to something, or in a certain way about something, . . . I know [that] is my genuine response. And I like that because I think I got so used to trying to control [my reactions] that sometimes I would believe the control and not the real thing. And I think once you're authentic, you draw people to you, and you inspire people that way." She has had friends tell her things like "I find the way you express yourself very endearing. You're just very open and honest about your emotions, and it's refreshing. And it forces me to be as well, even if I don't say it out loud." Adanna loves to see that she is having this positive impact on people, simply by being herself: "I feel like almost all my friendships are open and honest, which means there's less ambiguity, and the friendships . . . have real depth. And I like to feel that's having a positive impact. . . . Before, I wanted the same outcome of people [being] happy around me, but I was trying to almost puppet-master the whole thing. So I didn't have the real in-depth relationships."

She credits a lot of this growth in her relationships to the process of working through the ultimate questions. "One of my best friends from the MBA was someone [I'm very similar to]: very emotional and open people. We used to have all these conversations about our upbringing. He's Mexican. He's never had a Black friend. So, we seemed like we came from two very different places. But every time we talked to each other, it was like, 'Is this what talking to myself sounds like?' And we used to have these lunches, and we'd talk about anything: people in our lives who have died, what's important, unplanned deep questions. I loved the openness and vulnerability that came with that." And Adanna and her friend extended this discovery further: "We realized that it wasn't just us who were open to conversations like that; a lot of people were. I think that opened my eyes to the fact that you don't need to have known people for ten, twenty years to open up to them."

PETER

Peter's father taught him the importance of "baseline" respect for people: "My dad always says, 'Treat everyone the same, from the CEO to the janitor,' and that's something I've always felt is super important." In college, he gravitated to Immanuel Kant and his categorical imperative, an approach to generating moral insight through universalizable norms: All humans have equal moral worth and consideration, so any norms we act upon should give others the same weight as we give to ourselves (and everybody else). "If we treated everyone a certain way, or we took one thing and made it a rule, how would that affect the greater world? So I think [it's important to] treat people [the same] regardless of status and stature. That's something that was heavily imparted to me." Thus, Peter strives to treat everyone he meets with the same level of respect: "No matter who you meet, . . . you should always be pleasantly and respectfully interacting with them. I think there's a lot of disrespect that you find from people because of religion, political opinions, sports teams, things that they enjoy. . . . Treating everyone equally [means] that everyone deserves this baseline level of respect and humanity. I'm not obligated to like [them or] spend time with people who I don't have as much in common with, but that doesn't mean that they have less value than the people who I interact more with."

Peter is curious about people and eager to learn what they're interested in, and this has become more central to his approach to relationships as he's met more people: "As I got older, I started to identify more and branch out more. I met friends who like different things. When I started my first job, I fell in with a crowd of guys who loved watching football. So every Sunday we would go watch football. I had never done that before, and I was like, 'Oh my gosh! I'm gonna hate this.' But I ended up really loving it."

His openness has been really rewarding to him: "I think you can have a lot of deeper conversations with a broader group of people by being open to those experiences. Learning to ask questions of people when they show passion about something. Learning to lean in and try to learn about why they are passionate about that. . . . I feel like it's really helped my relationships get a lot richer with a lot broader experience [and a greater] number of people. I have so many people that when something happens in the world—be it sports, be it cultural, be it politics—that I can text a wide variety of people to have deep, fun, interesting conversations on those topics. Being open to what's meaningful to them is [how I build] relationships."

Robert, Joshua, Liniksha, Adanna, and Peter have all grown and changed in how they approach relationships—from letting themselves be vulnerable with people who previously seemed too different, to establishing boundaries with others and finding a relationship with themselves, to learning the joy of authentic conversation. As in all the chapters, their reflections are snapshots of particular moments in their lives. But as they make clear, even as their attitudes inevitably shift as they go through their lives, they will continue to consciously consider how they relate to other people. Through this process of ultimate questions, they keep themselves open to new insights and new possibilities.

WORKSHOP ACTIVITIES

ACTIVITY 1: Generate your four sentences on "How should we get along with others?"

- What are your four sentences on this question?
- As you look at your sentences, what do you notice? What sources do you think have most shaped your answer (for example, what your parents taught you, your religious upbringing, what you learned in school, what you learned from your friends)?

- Is this a good answer? Or do you already see a weakness in it in terms of helping you navigate a healthy relationship with people you see as other? What might you want from an answer that could improve on what you have? Where would that make a difference in your life?
- As you look at the growing division in the world, what needs to change to create more possibilities for people to "get along," even if they don't agree? How might your friendships, or your experience at school or work with people you currently see as other, become better if you could focus more on how they are like you rather than how wrong they are about this topic?
- Where is it critical for you to get things "right" and not compromise? Where are these other choices or options not just other legitimate ways to see this issue (e.g., believing in a specific religion), but wrong? Where does this feeling come from, and what might you do to better understand where to draw lines in the future? When do you need to stand up, make different choices, say things that others might reject or question?
- What would it take to change your mind, either to be more tolerant of others and their beliefs and behaviors or to become less so? How might your life, and how you get along with others, potentially start to shift in important ways? What can you do to test your intuition and start to make changes that allow you to create a different future for yourself and for others around you?

ACTIVITY 2: Revisit chapter 1 reflection

Turn back to activity 4 in chapter 1 and the questions you asked yourself as you worked through your answers to "Who are we?" and "Who am I?" Consider them from the viewpoint of another person. Better yet, open a new conversation with another person—maybe the same person you shared with back in chapter 1—and see how your and their answers may have changed.

ACTIVITY 3: **Enneagram, again**

Look at the Enneagram test again (see activity 5 from chapter 1), and use it not just to understand yourself but also to gain new perspectives on other people. Why do certain people and certain behaviors really draw you in and make you feel connected to others? And why do others really bother you and make you dislike or even hate others? Chances are that some of why you feel the way you do about others has to do with traits associated with your Enneagram number and how they either complement or clash with people who are aligned with their numbers. If you can use this tool as a way to understand and unpack where some of this tension comes from (and recognize that it isn't about them, but more about how your respective approaches to life interact), it can be easier to tolerate them rather than judge them. Such understanding can also give you options for how you interact with them. If you can expect certain behaviors, you are less surprised by them. You can take steps to avoid putting others in places where they do things that you dislike or that frustrate you, and you can shape how you interact with them in ways that bring out their (and your) better qualities.

ACTIVITY 4: **Talk with someone outside of your comfort zone**

- Try to find someone you see as other in a way that matters to you (e.g., you have different religious beliefs, you have different political views, or your skin color or sexual orientation is different). Try to find some time to talk with them and get to know them. Don't even dig into your difference yet. Just spend time talking with them, especially if you haven't before. Chances are you will find some things about them that are more like you, or you may find new areas where you disagree. How does that conversation change how you think about them?
- If you feel like things have gotten easier between you, can you start to dabble in the waters of the places where you disagree—where this "otherness" resides? Look at the guide to hard

conversations in appendix 1 of this book and consider especially how you might empathetically try to understand the other person and their views, and how you might avoid criticizing them, changing their minds, or talking about this difference in a way that highlights its otherness.

- Afterward, reflect on the conversation: Did it open up new ways of getting along, or at least interacting differently, that can ease some of the tension between you? Or did it reaffirm or deepen that sense of otherness and remind you how much you need more boundaries with them? How does the conversation change how you think about them?

EXTENDING THE CONVERSATION

You cannot hope to build a better world without improving the individuals. To that end each of us must work for his own improvement, and at the same time share a general responsibility for all humanity, our particular duty being to aid those to whom we think we can be most useful.

—**MARIE CURIE**, *Pierre Curie*

This book started with a basic premise: Ultimate questions are an intrinsic part of our lives even if we don't notice them. They are baked into our existence, and we can't help but have answers we live by. So the challenge isn't to create answers from scratch, but to recognize the answers we've already been using and to ask if they are our best answers, if they serve us and enable us to live the life we seek. At the same time, you might feel like the questions exist at a great distance from your daily life, making them difficult to engage with. They might seem vast and intimidating, leaving you with little idea of where to start or how to get to a "good" answer. And even as you begin the process of reflecting on these questions, you might find it daunting, or you might feel out of your depth and unable to make any real progress.

One of the goals of this book has been to soothe some of these fears and insecurities—and to help you overcome the impostor syndrome that prevents many of us from consciously thinking about these deep questions in the first place. I have tried to show that these are questions for all of us and that we all weigh in on them in the daily doing of our lives. We're not responsible for pushing the boundaries of human knowledge. We don't need to become philosophers, psychologists, or any other kinds of experts to face these questions. Our home can be ours even if we didn't build it from scratch. Tackling these questions is part of life for each of us, and we all have to cobble together answers as best we can in order to get on with our lives. Humility is important: It allows us to see that our efforts are imperfect and that our answers may change. But humility shouldn't mean we don't engage with these questions at all or that we hand them off to someone else. That's a bit like letting your parents tell you how to live, something most teenagers understand is a pretty bad idea—and one that won't generate answers that feel like yours. It is only when we do the work on our own that we can get to a place where we can claim the answers are ours, even if they end up being remarkably similar to the answers our parents lived out. In fact, it's an act of great humility to recognize that we already have answers and then to be able to share them with others. Only once we consciously recognize the answers we already live out can we acknowledge their imperfections and be open to the possibility of change.

I hope that reading this book brings you greater self-awareness and more willingness to consciously examine what might otherwise remain unconscious and fixed in place. Many of us have answers to ultimate questions that work pretty well, at least for the time being. We've absorbed the values of our family, friends, and community, and by accepting them we have led adequate lives that have allowed us to avoid jail, to stay in our families' good graces, and to keep out of the unemployment line. Yet few people would say that is enough, or that such an approach to life is truly living. If we just do what others expect us to without making choices of our own—if we go through life on autopilot—we miss out on the richness and possibility of a full life. Instead, when we become aware of the challenge of ultimate questions and realize that we have to own our choices, we can begin to see that the work of reflection has value. Even those of us who are generally happy with our lives and who feel content with our sense of purpose and identity can benefit from the invitation to reflect. In fact, we might come away from thinking about ultimate questions unchanged. If so, that's great! This work doesn't have to mean that your life and choices will change radically. Even if you end up coming back to the answers you currently have, the exercise has value: You will have a greater awareness of your answers and heightened understanding of where they've come from and why you believe them. In short, the process of reflecting on ultimate questions helps you see and embrace the terms on which you approach life, to see them as yours, however imperfect and unsatisfying some of those answers may be. They are the best you can do right now—and that's okay. It is better to know who you are and what you believe than to proceed on autopilot and only discover late in life how you wished you'd approached life. And this work also helps you better understand others, why they do what they do, and how you can create richer and better relationships with them.

I also hope that this greater self-awareness will keep you curious and open to growth. Part of the work of engaging with ultimate questions is recognizing that our answers to these questions change naturally as we navigate major life events—going to school, starting a relationship, beginning a career, and having children. Our values and identities rarely remain static. Consciously and intentionally thinking about these questions can help us navigate these changes in a way that feels authentic and organic, which also helps us see them as part of a larger whole. Holding our answers lightly, recognizing that they are not fully fixed, can keep us open to the influence of our life experiences. We don't know how much we can love someone until we find our life partner, or have a child, or say goodbye to a dear one. These key moments remind us of the value of deep reflection. And deep reflection, as part of our daily life, can make us feel better about our choices, if it allows us to believe that we truly have done our best.

But perhaps my greatest hope is that, by doing the work of this book, you'll learn how to enrich your connection with others. Ultimate questions structure the deepest conversations we can have with each other. They invite the greatest forms of intimacy and vulnerability. Through these conversations, we can share the deepest aspects of ourselves and get to know the deepest aspects of another person, which brings about more empathy and understanding. These kinds of connections are especially important in the domains of leadership and management. I hope that this book gives you some of the tools to have these conversations, and to do so in a way that feels both intimate and safe.

In service of this, I hope this work helps you embrace the collaborative aspect of these questions and understand that we never tackle them in isolation. You now have the resources to start thinking about these questions with others, whether that means having a "board of advisers" or staging informal check-ins with friends and loved ones. Our individual perspectives on these questions are often limited and riddled with blind spots, as are our perspectives on ourselves. We need the input of other people to help fill in the gaps when our closeness to our own lives blinkers us. Part of the work of reflection is simply having the humility to absorb other people's input and recognize that we often miss important things about ourselves.

We live in a world that is making it harder to have the conversations envisioned in this book. I see this on the news, but also in my own classroom. Whether it's national politics, international relations, or college discussions, people appear less willing to have deep and honest dialogue with others. In a world that is rapidly shrinking, one where so many of our biggest challenges require people from different groups to work together, it is vital that we move in the opposite direction. The stakes are high. One slim volume isn't likely to have much of an impact on this trajectory, but I hope that this book is part of a larger conversation that acknowledges our deep differences while still trying to chart a way for us to recognize and appreciate each other.

From my experience teaching the "Ultimate Questions" course, most of my students have come to see the power of the questions as what mattered most. They developed the ability to sharpen their minds, probe deeper into conversations, engage and understand others, and be alert for moments of real transition: moments that call not for just another minor, incremental change within the existing system but for people to question or change that system and how we think about it. And perhaps this applies not only to our own personal values, identity, and purpose, but also to those of our community, or nation, or world. Throughout much of the twentieth century, we in the "modern world" have celebrated our ability to "tolerate" differences without digging into what those differences really mean. That has often meant papering over differences that are real, that matter. And it has also meant implicitly elevating some groups of people by ceding to them the ability to control who is tolerated and who isn't, which points of view merit consideration and which don't. This bland and tepid tolerance has masked real conflicts in terms of whose beliefs are understood to matter and whose aren't. And it has functioned as an excuse to keep things largely the way they are and to suppress changes that many people desperately want. In the United States, for example, we celebrate the legal equality that allows (almost) everyone to weigh in on matters of public policy, but we tend to be quieter about the well-documented fact that those of us with lots of money also have much more influence over public policy than those of us without it.

And today, even that tepid tolerance seems to be breaking down. Perhaps our modern world demands a more robust coexistence, one that recognizes the real differences between us but treats them as sources of enrichment rather than as obstacles to be overcome, and that meaningfully distributes power to coordinate those differences so that we all truly do have the equal say that democracy is supposed to provide. We've yet to achieve a truly democratic society. A defining question of our time is whether we can. *Ultimate Questions* can't solve that challenge. But I end with the hope that, in its own very small way, this book contributes to the conversation. The four ultimate questions imply another question: Where do all the differences in our individual answers finally leave us?

APPENDIX 1

A GUIDE TO HAVING HARD CONVERSATIONS

OVERVIEW

This book invites you to start exploring territory that is exciting, yet also can be fear inducing—or at least might get your pulse up and make you partly uncomfortable. These are topics and conversations that matter; they involve revealing things about yourself and asking others to do the same. So approaching them well is important, as it enables you to learn the most from them and avoid having bad experiences that discourage you from continuing this kind of work.

My first choice would be to invite you into my classroom, where I can serve as a guide or resource—and you have peers to turn to if things start to go sideways. Unfortunately, that isn't an option here. What I lay out in this appendix is a set of tools to help you approach these conversations and activities in ways that can shrink the risk and make it more likely that the experience will be positive. They are imperfect, they are limited, and they won't guarantee that you will have a positive experience in your conversation—any such promise would be empty since there are no foolproof ways to have these conversations. That said, sometimes having a bad conversation (or one that feels like a setback or failure) can be a good thing. With the right mindset, mistakes become opportunities to learn.

With that in mind, here are some tips to help you approach the conversations so you can get the most out of them and avoid things that can get in the way.

FRAMING MATTERS

How you frame or phrase your topic can either heighten the tension or make it far easier to have a civil and thoughtful conversation. Take a step back from the conversation you think you want to have and make sure the words and phrases you use won't be a provocation to your conversation partner. Think about how your partner might want to frame the conversation and see if you can come at it in ways that are less good/bad, right/wrong, us/them, and more about what you have in common. I often tell my students that the best way to talk about ultimate questions is *not* to tell the other person, "We are going to talk about ultimate questions." That framing sounds analytical and imposing to most people, and it might make them want to run away from the discussion even if they like and trust you. A much better way into the conversation is to ask a mundane and relatable question like "What do you enjoy most about your life [or work or relationships]?" or "What do you value most in friendships?" If you are a leader or manager in the workplace, you might ask, "How can I best advocate for you when I make leadership decisions that affect you?" Questions like these meet people where they are, allow them to speak to what they know and care about, and tend not to overwhelm them. Trying to tackle "Who are we as humans and why are we here?" tends to make most people's eyes glaze over unless and until you find a way to make that topic more accessible, more relatable, and something they are already doing.

BE CURIOUS, LISTEN, AND LEARN

The best way to get someone interested in a conversation is by expressing curiosity—showing genuine interest in them and what they have to say.

That means listening to them and being willing to learn from them. Being empathetic and invested in hearing what another person has to say is a powerful way to show your commitment to them and the fidelity of the conversation. Be conscious of how much of the time you are talking as well as what you are saying so you can make sure that you are listening more than talking—and that when you do talk, you are doing so not to share your own answers but to dig deeper into the other person's thoughts and why they have them.

MODEL AND CONVEY EMPATHY

Both in how we speak and in how we present ourselves, it is critical to express empathy. This doesn't mean you become a blank slate, ready to toss out your own beliefs and latch on to those of the person on the other side of the table. Being empathetic means putting your views to the side (for the moment) in order to show a genuine interest in what the other person believes and why they believe it. You should be asking questions and engaging with them, yet it is vital you do so with the goal of understanding them and their views—not pressing them, challenging them, or (implicitly or explicitly) attacking what they believe.

AVOID JUDGMENT AND ATTACKS

Discussing hard topics on which we disagree is already difficult enough—and doesn't really need a conversation. On some topics (e.g., whether we are "red" or "blue" in US politics), we would rather hide our cards than share. Expressing judgment and attacking the person you're talking with are ideal ways to shut down conversation and build animosity. To have hard conversations, you need to be willing to suspend your judgment about the other person's views and refrain from attacking them—and to consider what you are saying and the language that you use from their perspective. Often, we are so used to seeing an issue from the standpoint of our own group that we don't recognize how the language we use carries a built-in implicit judgment of others' views.

DON'T TRY TO EDUCATE OR CONDESCEND

When you disagree with someone, especially when it comes to hard topics like politics or religion, entering a conversation with the intent to change them (or their point of view) is a recipe for disaster. Not only does this not change anyone's mind, but it tends to backfire by further entrenching people in their views.

EXPRESS A WILLINGNESS TO CONSIDER OTHER VIEWS AND CHANGE YOUR MIND

Given new information, compelling data, powerful personal experiences, or deep internal reflection, we all should be willing to reconsider and even revise our views. Take time to ask yourself, "What it would take to change my mind?" If the answer is "nothing," then you are closing off parts of your life and beliefs to the kind of inquiry this book invites. Even with our most cherished and deeply held beliefs, we should be willing to make changes and updates, given the right circumstances. Especially at the beginning, it may be hard to open some beliefs to that kind of examination, so don't try to go too fast too soon. Yet, as you get into the work, you may well find it freeing and powerful to recognize that your beliefs are just that—beliefs. It can make them more precious and more uniquely yours to acknowledge their contingency.

GET COMFORTABLE BEING UNCOMFORTABLE

Having hard conversations on deep topics is inherently challenging. There is no way to fully gauge how hard any of these topics will be for you until you try it. That said, you should aim to tackle something that will stretch you and take you (at least a bit) outside your comfort zone. If it doesn't, then you need to find another topic or experience to share with others or lean further into what is potentially risky for you—for example, admitting you don't know something; sharing stories that reveal something personal about you to others you don't know well; or having an experience that makes you uncomfortable, like a worship service of a religion you don't believe in, and then talking about it. I tell my students, using the analogy of someone learning to swim, "Don't hang out in the kiddie pool, since there isn't anything there that is risky for you; but don't jump into the deep end until you've learned a good bit about how to swim." Only you can judge what level of challenge will get your heart going or make you think twice about doing something (without it being truly terrifying). Over time, you will develop a knack for knowing yourself and what you can handle—and you will get more comfortable with being uncomfortable. Too much too soon can make it hard to enjoy this work or reap its benefits. You need to have some people looking out for you, like a leader at a religious or political gathering, or a conversation partner willing to shift gears or stop if it gets too uncomfortable. If you are intentional and build in the guardrails up front, it gets easier to dip your body into the water and start moving out of the shallow end.

WATCH FOR NONVERBAL CUES

Beyond your intentions and these guides, you should be looking for other cues about how things are going. If you are really present in the discussion and engage your emotional intelligence, chances are you will notice how the other person is responding so you can adapt accordingly. Be on the lookout for cues like the kind of language they use (direct and divisive, neutral and impartial, or welcoming and agreeable, for example), their tone of voice (have they gotten very quiet? Is their voice getting louder?), and their body language (do they look tense? Are they shrinking and looking submissive or uncomfortable? Do they seem open and relaxed?).

Particularly if things are becoming more intense or confrontational, use that data to redirect the conversation and your approach. Find another way into the conversation, spend more time asking them questions about what they think, or redirect the topic to things that are safer or on which you agree. Sometimes you can get into very deep conversations right away—and with other folks, you may find it challenging to get beyond the surface. While you should want to push the boundaries, it's important to make sure the others in the conversation are okay with it and willing to move into deeper waters.

BE WILLING TO ACCEPT THAT SOME CONVERSATIONS CAN'T (AND SHOULDN'T) HAPPEN

Especially if you fundamentally disagree with someone on topics that you both are deeply passionate about, you may find it hard to use these tools to have a good conversation on certain topics. For instance, when it comes to US politics, if the other person is deeply "red" and you are deeply "blue," it is quite possible that you won't be able to have a constructive conversation about the next election. That said, there are many other conversations you can get into related to politics and things that matter to you both that may be easier for you to manage—especially if you follow the guidelines in this appendix.

ACTIVITIES TO TRY, EITHER BY YOURSELF OR WITH OTHERS

You can do much of the work in this book on your own. At the same time, some of the most powerful ways to learn and grow through this work are through engaging with others. In my class, while I put a lot of weight on individual reflection and writing, perhaps the most impactful part of the course happens in the students' "salon groups." To make this work more challenging, I don't allow them to choose their groups. Instead,

I pass out a pre-class survey about their values and attitudes, then I use those answers to design groups of five or six that include members who think differently from each other. As teams, they craft four group activities and conversations, and then post about them on the course web page so others can see what different teams are doing and how the experience went.

Some examples:

- Go to a worship service of a religion you don't believe in, and then talk with each other about the experience. You can also make time to read about the service[1] or talk to someone who is part of that religious community beforehand (to know what it will be like and how to fit in—or at least be respectful and not stick out) and afterward to learn more about what you experienced.
- Have a conversation over drinks about how you were raised, what you were taught to believe about how the world came into being, what kind of creatures we are and why we ended up here, whether there is a God or gods, and so on. Rather than asking each person "Do you believe in God? Why or why not?," this lets group members decide what they want to share about their lives and how they want to phrase that experience (e.g., I am religious, spiritual, agnostic, atheist).
- Arrange a meeting with someone who has strong views on a topic that likely differ from yours (and those of at least some other members of your group) and talk with that person about it, then debrief as a group after the meeting.
- Watch or listen to media that ventures into challenging territory and could spark hard conversations about topics you care about. Examples might include:
  - Watching the movie *The Big Sick* and discussing the challenge of finding a marriage partner when your parents feel strongly that you should marry within your religious or cultural background.

- Watching a recent episode of a newscast covering a current conflict in the world—or even better, watching two or three different news shows—and discussing how this coverage shapes how we see and think about the issues.
- Listening to a podcast like *Hidden Brain* that covers issues that stretch or challenge our views of who we are as humans and how we connect to each other and the world, then discussing it.
- Watching a few YouTube videos of Dr. Frans de Waal working with primates, then talking about this with the group.
- Watching the film *Nomadland* or the documentary *Working: What We Do All Day* and talking about work today as well as the future of work. What kind of work do we want and should we have—and why don't we have it? How can we find (or make) better work?

APPENDIX 2

RESOURCES

ON HAVING HARD CONVERSATIONS

Brackett, Marc. *Permission to Feel: The Power of Emotional Intelligence to Achieve Well-Being and Success.* Celadon, 2020.

Brooks, David. *How to Know a Person: The Art of Seeing Others Deeply and Being Deeply Seen.* Random House, 2023.

Grenny, Joseph, Kerry Patterson, Ron McMillan, Al Switzler, and Emily Gregory. *Crucial Conversations: Tools for Talking When Stakes Are High.* McGraw Hill, 2021.

Kross, Ethan. *Shift: Managing Your Emotions—So They Don't Manage You.* Crown, 2025.

Leslie, Ian. *Conflicted: How Productive Disagreements Lead to Better Outcomes.* Harper Business, 2021.

Stone, Douglas, Bruce Patton, and Sheila Heen. *Difficult Conversations: How to Discuss What Matters Most.* Penguin Books, 2023.

Ury, William. *Possible: How We Survive (and Thrive) in an Age of Conflict.* Harper Business, 2024.

CHAPTER 1

Tests for thinking about "Who am I?"

16Personalities. Personality test. https://www.16personalities.com/.

Brown, Brené. "Daring Leadership Assessment." Dare to Lead Hub. https://daretolead.brenebrown.com/assessment/.

Truity. "The Big Five Personality Test." https://www.truity.com/test/big-five-personality-test.

Truity. "The Enneagram Personality Test." https://www.truity.com/test/enneagram-personality-test-super.

Resources to guide self-exploration/write your own story

Brown, Brené, host. *Unlocking Us*. Vox Media Podcast Network. Podcast. https://brenebrown.com/podcast-show/unlocking-us/.

Cameron, Julia. *The Artist's Way: A Spiritual Path to Higher Creativity*. 25th anniversary ed. TarcherPerigee, 2016.

David, Susan. *Emotional Agility: Get Unstuck, Embrace Change, and Thrive in Work and Life*. Avery, 2016.

David, Susan. "The Gift and Power of Emotional Courage." TED Talk, New Orleans, November 2017. Video, 16 min., 38 sec. https://www.ted.com/talks/susan_david_the_gift_and_power_of_emotional_courage.

Davidson, Richard J., and Sharon Begley. *The Emotional Life of Your Brain: How Its Unique Patterns Affect the Way You Think, Feel, and Live—and How You Can Change Them*. Illustrated ed. Avery, 2012.

Goldberg, Natalie. *Writing Down the Bones: Freeing the Writer Within*. 2nd ed. Shambhala Publications, 2005.

Gottlieb, Lori. *Maybe You Should Talk to Someone: A Therapist, Her Therapist, and Our Lives Revealed*. Harper, 2019.

Gottlieb, Lori. *Maybe You Should Talk to Someone: The Workbook; A Toolkit for Editing Your Story and Changing Your Life*. PESI Publishing, 2021.

Grosz, Stephen. *The Examined Life: How We Lose and Find Ourselves*. W. W. Norton & Company, 2014.

Intelligent Change. "The Five Minute Journal." https://www.intelligentchange.com/products/the-five-minute-journal.

Lamott, Anne. *Bird by Bird: Some Instructions on Writing and Life*. Anchor Books, 2019.

Neff, Kristin. "Self-Compassion Practices." https://self-compassion.org/category/exercises/.

Patel, Meera Lee. *Start Where You Are: A Journal for Self-Exploration*. Perigee, 2015.

Models of self-exploration/resources that show others engaging in this question

Cain, Susan. *Quiet: The Power of Introverts in a World That Can't Stop Talking*. Crown, 2012.

Doyle, Glennon. *Untamed*. Dial Press, 2020.

Doyle, Glennon, Abby Wambach, and Amanda Doyle, hosts. *We Can Do Hard Things*. Audacy. Podcast. http://wecandohardthingspodcast.com/.

Gay, Roxane. *Hunger: A Memoir of (My) Body*. Harper, 2017.

Grant, Adam. *Originals: How Non-Conformists Move the World*. Viking, 2016.

Karr, Mary. *The Liars' Club: A Memoir*. 10th anniversary ed. Penguin Books, 2005.

McInerny, Nora. *Terrible, Thanks for Asking*. Feelings & Co. Podcast. https://feelingsand.co/podcasts/terrible-thanks-for-asking/.

Morrison, Toni. "The Site of Memory." In *Inventing the Truth: The Art and Craft of Memoir*, 2nd ed., edited by William Zinsser. Houghton Mifflin, 1995.

The Moth. Podcast. https://themoth.org/podcast.

Sale, Anna, host. *Death, Sex & Money*. WNYC Studios. Podcast. https://www.wnycstudios.org/shows/deathsexmoney.

Sale, Anna. *Let's Talk About Hard Things: Death, Sex, Money, and Other Difficult Conversations*. Simon & Schuster, 2021.

StoryCorps. https://storycorps.org/.

Resources for exploring family

FamilySearch. https://www.familysearch.org/en/.

Genealogy.com. https://www.genealogy.com/.

Genealogy.com. "Get Nosy with Aunt Rosie: Example Questions for Oral Histories." https://www.genealogy.com/articles/research/70_tipsoral.html.

Jacobs, A. J. *It's All Relative: Adventures Up and Down the World's Family Tree*. Simon & Schuster, 2017.

McGoldrick, Monica. *You Can Go Home Again: Reconnecting with Your Family*. W. W. Norton & Company, 1995.

Ritchie, Donald A. *Doing Oral History: A Practical Guide*. 2nd ed. Oxford University Press, 2003.

Resources for thinking about who we are as humans

Ariely, Dan. *Predictably Irrational, Revised and Expanded Edition: The Hidden Forces That Shape Our Decisions*. Harper Perennial, 2010.

Bloom, Paul. *Just Babies: The Origins of Good and Evil*. Crown, 2013.

Damasio, Antonio. *Descartes' Error: Emotion, Reason, and the Human Brain*. Illustrated ed. Penguin Books, 2005.

Eagleman, David. *Incognito: The Secret Lives of the Brain*. Illustrated ed. Vintage, 2012.

Greenblatt, Stephen. *The Swerve: How the World Became Modern*. W. W. Norton & Company, 2012.

Haidt, Jonathan. *The Righteous Mind: Why Good People Are Divided by Politics and Religion*. Vintage Books, 2013.

Harari, Yuval Noah. *Sapiens: A Brief History of Humankind*. Illustrated ed. Harper, 2015.

Kahneman, Daniel. *Thinking, Fast and Slow*. Farrar, Straus and Giroux, 2011.

Kaufman, Scott Barry, host. *The Psychology Podcast*. iHeartRadio. https://scottbarrykaufman.com/podcast/.

Roughley, Neil. "Human Nature." *Stanford Encyclopedia of Philosophy* (spring 2021). https://plato.stanford.edu/archives/spr2021/entries/human-nature/.

Sacks, Oliver. *The Man Who Mistook His Wife for a Hat and Other Clinical Tales*. Summit Books, 1985.

Classic texts that explore the human condition

Freud, Sigmund, and Paul Keegan. *The Psychopathology of Everyday Life*. Translated by Anthea Bell. Penguin Books, 2003.

James, William. *The Varieties of Religious Experience: A Study in Human Nature*. Modern Library, 1999.

Montaigne, Michel de. *Michel de Montaigne: The Complete Essays*. Translated and edited with an introduction and notes by M. A. Screech. Reprint ed. Penguin Books, 1993.

Nin, Anaïs. *Fire: From "A Journal of Love"; The Unexpurgated Diary of Anaïs Nin, 1934–1937*. Mariner Books, 1996.

Woolf, Virginia. *Mrs. Dalloway*. With a foreword by Maureen Howard. Mariner Classics, 1990.

CHAPTER 2

Resources for thinking about your personal strengths

Csikszentmihalyi, Mihaly. *Flow: The Psychology of Optimal Experience*. Harper Perennial Modern Classics, 2008.

Epstein, David. *Range: Why Generalists Triumph in a Specialized World*. Riverhead Books, 2021.

Gallup. "CliftonStrengths." Online test. https://www.gallup.com/cliftonstrengths/en/252137/home.aspx.

Gardner, Howard. *Frames of Mind: The Theory of Multiple Intelligences*. 3rd ed. Basic Books, 2011.

Seligman, Martin E. P. *Authentic Happiness: Using the New Positive Psychology to Realize Your Potential for Lasting Fulfillment*. Reprint ed. Atria Books, 2004.

Seligman, Martin E. P. *Flourish*. Free Press, 2011.

The VIA Institute on Character. "Who Are You at Your Best?" Online test. https://www.viacharacter.org/.

Resources for thinking about purpose in work

Botton, Alain de. "A Kinder, Gentler Philosophy of Success." TED Talk, Oxford, England, July 2009. Video, 16 min., 37 sec. https://www.ted.com/talks/alain_de_botton_a_kinder_gentler_philosophy_of_success.

Botton, Alain de. *The Pleasures and Sorrows of Work*. Vintage, 2010.

Brown, Brené. "Dare to Lead Hub." https://daretolead.brenebrown.com/.

Brown, Brené. *Dare to Lead: Brave Work. Tough Conversations. Whole Hearts.* Random House, 2018.

Brown, Brené, host. *Dare to Lead*. Podcast. https://brenebrown.com/podcast-show/dare-to-lead/.

Callard, Agnes. *Aspiration: The Agency of Becoming*. Oxford University Press, 2018.

Crawford, Matthew B. *Shop Class as Soulcraft: An Inquiry into the Value of Work*. Reprint ed. Penguin Books, 2010.

García, Héctor, and Francesc Miralles. *Ikigai: The Japanese Secret to a Long and Happy Life*. Penguin Books, 2017.

Grant, Adam, host. *WorkLife with Adam Grant: A TED Original Podcast*. TED Conferences, LLC, and Transmitter Media. https://www.ted.com/podcasts/worklife.

Huffington, Arianna. *Thrive: The Third Metric to Redefining Success and Creating a Life of Well-Being, Wisdom, and Wonder*. Reprint ed. Harmony Books, 2015.

Pink, Daniel H. *Drive: The Surprising Truth About What Motivates Us*. Riverhead Books, 2011.

Resources for thinking about meaning of life/existence

Hall, Edith. *Aristotle's Way: How Ancient Wisdom Can Change Your Life*. Illustrated ed. Penguin Press, 2019.

Kalanithi, Paul. *When Breath Becomes Air*. With a foreword by Abraham Verghese. Random House, 2016.

Kaufman, Scott Barry. *Transcend: The New Science of Self-Actualization*. Illustrated ed. TarcherPerigee, 2020.

Tippett, Krista, host. *On Being with Krista Tippett*. On Being Studios. Podcast. https://onbeing.org/series/podcast/.

Ward, Pendleton, dir. *The Midnight Gospel*. Released April 20, 2020, on Netflix. https://www.netflix.com/title/80987903.

Classic texts about purpose/meaning

Aristotle. *Nicomachean Ethics*. Translated by Terence Irwin. 3rd ed. Hackett Publishing Company, Inc., 2019.

Campbell, Joseph. *The Hero with a Thousand Faces*. 3rd ed. New World Library, 2008.

Emerson, Ralph Waldo. *Self-Reliance*. CreateSpace Independent Publishing Platform, 2017.

Frankl, Viktor E. *Man's Search for Meaning*. Translated by Ilse Lasch. With a foreword by Harold S. Kushner and an afterword by William J. Winslade. Beacon Press, 2006.

Kierkegaard, Søren. *The Sickness unto Death: A Christian Psychological Exposition for Upbuilding and Awakening*. Edited and translated by Edna H. Hong and Howard V. Hong. Princeton University Press, 1983.

Kierkegaard, Søren. *Either/Or: A Fragment of Life*. Edited by Victor Eremita and translated by Alastair Hannay. Abridged ed. Penguin Books, 1992.

Merton, Thomas. *The Seven Storey Mountain: An Autobiography of Faith*. Mariner Books, 1999.

Niebuhr, Reinhold. *The Nature and Destiny of Man: A Christian Interpretation*. Westminster John Knox Press, 1996.

Pascal, Blaise. *Pensées*. Translated by A. J. Krailsheimer. Revised ed. Penguin Classics, 1995.

Thoreau, Henry David. *Walden and Civil Disobedience*. Penguin Classics, 1983.

Tolstoy, Leo. *A Confession*. Translated by Aylmer Maude and Louise Maude. CreateSpace Independent Publishing Platform, 2017.

CHAPTER 3

Resources for readers to actualize a good (better) life

Brach, Tara. "Guided Meditations." https://www.tarabrach.com/guided-meditations/.

Brach, Tara. *Radical Compassion: Learning to Love Yourself and Your World with the Practice of RAIN*. Penguin Life, 2020.

Brackett, Mark. *Permission to Feel: The Power of Emotional Intelligence to Achieve Well-Being and Success*. Celadon, 2020.

Brooks, David. *The Second Mountain: The Quest for a Moral Life*. Random House, 2019.

Burnett, Bill, and Dave Evans. *Designing Your Life: How to Build a Well-Lived, Joyful Life*. Knopf, 2016.

Dalai Lama [Tenzin Gyatso] and Desmond Tutu. *The Book of Joy: Lasting Happiness in a Changing World*. With Douglas Abrams. Illustrated ed. Avery, 2016.

Hanson, Rick. *Hardwiring Happiness: The New Brain Science of Contentment, Calm, and Confidence*. Illustrated ed. Harmony Books, 2013.

Kabat-Zinn, Jon. Guided meditations. https://jonkabat-zinn.com/.

Kornfield, Jack, host. Podcasts. https://jackkornfield.com/category/podcasts/.

Kornfield, Jack. "Mindfulness Meditation: The Fundamentals." https://jackkornfield.com/sp/mindfulness-meditation-the-fundamentals/.

McGonigal, Jane. *SuperBetter: The Power of Living Gamefully*. Reprint ed. Penguin Books, 2016.

Mindsight Institute. Series of online courses. https://www.mindsightinstitute.com.

Nhat Hanh, Thich. *Peace Is Every Step: The Path of Mindfulness in Everyday Life*. Ebury Publishing, 2010. eBook.

Pink, Daniel H. *The Power of Regret: How Looking Backward Moves Us Forward.* Riverhead Books, 2022.

Shapiro, Shauna. "The Power of Mindfulness: What You Practice Grows Stronger." TED Talk, New York, October 2016. Video, 13 min., 45 sec. https://www.youtube.com/watch?v=IeblJdB2-Vo.

Shapiro, Shauna L., and Linda E. Carlson. *The Art and Science of Mindfulness: Integrating Mindfulness into Psychology and the Helping Professions.* 2nd ed. American Psychological Association, 2017.

SuperBetter. Game. https://v1.superbetter.com/want_to_play.

Resources on the science of happiness

Gilbert, Daniel. *Stumbling on Happiness*. Vintage, 2007.

Goleman, Daniel, and Richard J. Davidson. *Altered Traits: Science Reveals How Meditation Changes Your Mind, Brain, and Body*. Illustrated ed. Avery, 2017.

Goleman, Daniel, Hanuman Goleman, and Elizabeth Solomon, hosts. *First Person Plural: EI & Beyond*. Key Step Media. Podcast. https://www.keystepmedia.com/first-person-plural/.

Haidt, Jonathan. *The Happiness Hypothesis: Finding Modern Truth in Ancient Wisdom*. Basic Books, 2006.

Salzberg, Sharon. *Real Happiness: The Power of Meditation; A 28-Day Program*. Workman Publishing Company, Inc., 2010.

Salzberg, Sharon, host. *Metta Hour with Sharon Salzberg*. Podcast. https://www.sharonsalzberg.com/metta-hour-podcast/.

Santos, Laurie, host. *The Happiness Lab with Dr. Laurie Santos*. Pushkin. Podcast. https://www.happinesslab.fm.

Seppälä, Emma. *The Happiness Track: How to Apply the Science of Happiness to Accelerate Your Success*. Reprint ed. HarperOne, 2017.

Personal journeys toward the good life

Happier. Meditation app. https://www.meditatehappier.com/.

Harris, Dan. *10% Happier: How I Tamed the Voice in My Head, Reduced Stress Without Losing My Edge, and Found Self-Help That Actually Works—A True Story*. Reprint ed. Dey Street Books, 2014.

Harris, Dan, host. *10% Happier with Dan Harris*. iHeart. Podcast. https://www.iheart.com/podcast/867-10-happier-with-dan-harris-28888874/.

Linsky, Max, host. *70 over 70*. Pineapple Street Studios. Podcast. https://pineapple.fm/70-over-70.

Rubin, Gretchen. Articles. https://gretchenrubin.com/articles/.

Rubin, Gretchen. *The Happiness Project: Or, Why I Spent a Year Trying to Sing in the Morning, Clean My Closets, Fight Right, Read Aristotle, and Generally Have More Fun*. Revised ed. Harper Paperbacks, 2015.

Contemporary reflections on what the good life means today

Odell, Jenny. *How to Do Nothing: Resisting the Attention Economy*. Melville House, 2019.

Pollan, Michael. *How to Change Your Mind: What the New Science of Psychedelics Teaches Us About Consciousness, Dying, Addiction, Depression, and Transcendence*. Penguin Press, 2018.

Smith, Zadie. "Joy." *New York Review of Books*, January 10, 2013. https://www.nybooks.com/articles/2013/01/10/joy/?srsltid=AfmBOorBPWxoVonmbUy8HM63cydKMj7eHIHvoinXzuDZ5H3Fa6s6NnMQ.

Solomon, Patrick Takaya, dir. *Finding Joe*. Posted March 19, 2020, by Patrick Solomon. YouTube video, 1 hr., 20 min. https://www.youtube.com/watch?v=s8nFACrLxro.

Contemporary takes on the good life that draw on philosophy

Botton, Alain de. *The Consolations of Philosophy*. Reprint ed. Vintage, 2001.

Holiday, Ryan, host. *The Daily Stoic Podcast*. Wondery. https://dailystoic.com/podcast/.

Kaag, John. *Hiking with Nietzsche: On Becoming Who You Are.* Farrar, Straus and Giroux, 2018.

Pigliucci, Massimo. *How to Be a Stoic: Using Ancient Philosophy to Live a Modern Life.* Basic Books, 2017.

Puett, Michael, and Christine Gross-Loh. *The Path: What Chinese Philosophers Can Teach Us About the Good Life.* Reprint ed. Simon & Schuster, 2017.

Wilson, Catherine. *How to Be an Epicurean: The Ancient Art of Living Well.* Basic Books, 2019.

Classic texts on the good life

Aristotle. *Nicomachean Ethics.* Translated by Terence Irwin. 3rd ed. Hackett Publishing Company, Inc., 2019.

Aurelius, Marcus. *Meditations.* Translated by Martin Hammond with an introduction by Diskin Clay. Annotated ed. Penguin Classics, 2006.

Epicurus. *The Art of Happiness.* Translated by George K. Strodach with a foreword by Daniel Klein. Reissue ed. Penguin Classics, 2012.

Mill, John Stuart. *Utilitarianism.* CreateSpace Independent Publishing Platform, 2010.

Nietzsche, Friedrich. *Thus Spoke Zarathustra: A Book for Everyone and No One.* Translated and with an introduction and notes by R. J. Hollingdale. Penguin Classics, 1961.

The Republic of Plato. Translated by Allan Bloom with an introduction by Adam Kirsch. 3rd edition. Basic Books, 2016.

CHAPTER 4

Resources for thinking about communities big and small

Boo, Katherine. *Behind the Beautiful Forevers: Life, Death, and Hope in a Mumbai Undercity.* Reprint ed. Random House Trade Paperbacks, 2014.

Putnam, Robert D. *Bowling Alone: The Collapse and Revival of American Community.* Touchstone Books by Simon & Schuster, 2001.

Solnit, Rebecca. *A Paradise Built in Hell: The Extraordinary Communities That Arise in Disaster*. Penguin Books, 2010.

Resources for thinking about altruism and empathy

Grant, Adam. *Give and Take: Why Helping Others Drives Our Success*. Reprint ed. Penguin Books, 2014.

Jamison, Leslie. *The Empathy Exams: Essays*. Graywolf Press, 2014.

Raihani, Nichola. *The Social Instinct: How Cooperation Shaped the World*. St. Martin's Press, 2021.

Ricard, Matthieu. *Altruism: The Power of Compassion to Change Yourself and the World*. Little, Brown and Company, 2015.

Waal, Frans de. *The Age of Empathy: Nature's Lessons for a Kinder Society*. Souvenir Press, 2011.

Philosophical takes on coexistence and obligation to others

Rawls, John. *A Theory of Justice*. Revised ed. Belknap Press of Harvard University Press, 1999.

Rousseau, Jean-Jacques. *The Social Contract*. CreateSpace Independent Publishing Platform, 2014.

Sandel, Michael J. *The Tyranny of Merit: What's Become of the Common Good?* Farrar, Straus and Giroux, 2020.

Singer, Peter. *The Life You Can Save: How to Do Your Part to End World Poverty*. Reprint ed. Random House Trade Paperbacks, 2010.

Stepan, Alfred, and Charles Taylor, eds. *Boundaries of Toleration*. Columbia University Press, 2014.

Resources for thinking about race and otherness

Baldwin, James. *The Fire Next Time*. Modern Library, 2021.

Coates, Ta-Nehisi. *Between the World and Me*. One World, 2015.

Code Switch. NPR. Podcast. https://www.npr.org/podcasts/510312/codeswitch.

Du Bois, W. E. B. *The Souls of Black Folk*. Reprint ed. Dover Publications, 1994.

Oluo, Ijeoma. *So You Want to Talk About Race*. Seal Press, 2019.

Rankine, Claudia. *Citizen: An American Lyric*. Graywolf Press, 2014.

Rankine, Claudia. *Just Us: An American Conversation*. Illustrated ed. Graywolf Press, 2020.

Tatum, Beverly Daniel. *Why Are All the Black Kids Sitting Together in the Cafeteria? And Other Conversations About Race*. Revised ed. Basic Books, 2017.

Wilkerson, Isabel. *The Warmth of Other Suns: The Epic Story of America's Great Migration*. Reprint ed. Vintage, 2011.

Miscellaneous dimensions of otherness (political, national, ethnic)

Anderson, Benedict. *Imagined Communities: Reflections on the Origin and Spread of Nationalism*. Revised ed. Verso, 2016.

Appiah, Kwame Anthony. *Cosmopolitanism: Ethics in a World of Strangers*. Illustrated ed. W. W. Norton & Company, 2007.

Appiah, Kwame Anthony. *The Lies That Bind: Rethinking Identity*. Illustrated ed. Liveright, 2019.

Bishop, Bill. *The Big Sort: Why the Clustering of Like-Minded America Is Tearing Us Apart*. Mariner Books, 2009.

Hochschild, Arlie Russell. *Strangers in Their Own Land: Anger and Mourning on the American Right*. The New Press, 2018.

Marron, Dylan, host. *Conversations with People Who Hate Me*. TED Audio Collective. Podcast. https://www.dylanmarron.com/podcast.

Mason, Lilliana. *Uncivil Agreement: How Politics Became Our Identity*. Illustrated ed. University of Chicago Press, 2018.

Navigating relationships with intimate others

Brown, Brené. "The Power of Vulnerability." TED Talk, Houston, June 2010. Video, 20 min., 2 sec. https://www.ted.com/talks/brene_brown_the_power_of_vulnerability.

Buber, Martin. *I And Thou*. Translated by Walter Kaufmann. 100th anniversary reissue. Free Press, 1971.

The Gottman Institute, Inc. *Gottman Card Decks*. Card-game app for couples. Released 2023. iOS 13.0 or later.

Johnson, Sue. *Hold Me Tight: Seven Conversations for a Lifetime of Love*. Little, Brown Spark, 2008.

Johnson, Susan. "Hold Me Tight Online." Online course for couples. https://holdmetightonline.com/.

Lerner, Harriet. *The Dance of Anger: A Woman's Guide to Changing the Patterns of Intimate Relationships*. Reprint ed. William Morrow Paperbacks, 2014.

Perel, Esther. *Mating in Captivity: Unlocking Erotic Intelligence*. Reprint ed. Harper Paperbacks, 2017.

Perel, Esther, host. *How's Work? with Esther Perel*. Esther Perel Global Media. https://open.spotify.com/show/0P13JasQfVZ1RiDCMZMYNU.

Perel, Esther, host. *Where Should We Begin? with Esther Perel*. Esther Perel Global Media. Podcast. https://www.estherperel.com/podcast.

Perel, Esther. "Where Should We Begin—A Game of Stories." 2nd ed. Game. https://www.estherperel.com/where-should-we-begin-the-game.

Prest, Kaitlin, host. *The Heart*. Radiotopia. Podcast. https://www.theheartradio.org.

Savage, Dan, host. *Savage Lovecast*. Podcast. https://www.savagelovecast.com/.

Sow, Aminatou, and Ann Friedman, hosts. *Call Your Girlfriend*. Podcast. https://www.callyourgirlfriend.com.

Strayed, Cheryl, and Steve Almond, hosts. *Dear Sugars*. WBUR. Podcast. https://www.wbur.org/podcasts/dearsugar.

ACKNOWLEDGMENTS

There are so many people to thank for making this book come to life.

The person I am most grateful to is my wife, Cathy. Not only is she an incredible human and life partner, but I don't think I would have come up with the idea for the "Ultimate Questions" course (and this book) without listening to her and digging into the topics that bridged our respective interests (hers are in life coaching using Jungian psychology). Her work helped deepen my sense not only that the ultimate questions are highly relevant for everyone, but that this work is essential to help people see how much of their lives is dictated by their current answers to the questions. She was there when I generated the first outline of the book on that beach on the Big Island of Hawaii on our tenth wedding anniversary, and she has been a great champion of these ideas and getting them out to the larger community. She has also, practically, made it possible for me to do this work, to harness what is left of my intellect, creativity, and energy to get this far. Without her I could easily have become dark and despondent, turning inward and feeding my own fear and anger. Instead, I have channeled much of that energy into a project that feels like the culmination of my career. This book, in many ways, encapsulates what was in my own mind as a child, the questions that seemed to hold me hostage at times (lying in bed at night at the age of eight, sweating and wrestling over the question of whether God existed). As I grew older and ventured into college, I realized that I wasn't a pure philosopher or theologian. I wanted to think about questions that mattered for how we live our everyday lives. That is what led me to graduate school and to my career as a professor at a business school—not something I could have predicted as a kid (or even most of the way through college). Yet, as I look back, it feels like exactly what I was seeking. Cathy helped me to come full circle—to bring the inspiration that began in my childhood into a book I can share with you.

I also want to thank my coauthors, Alex Bleiberg and John Nolan. They both played important roles in the creation of this book, and their influence is felt throughout. I was extremely fortunate to find such talented research assistants and partners in this project. I first started trying to write this book when John was my RA. While he helped me on several different projects, most of his work was related to ultimate questions. I'm extremely grateful to John for his hard work, dedication, collaboration, and impact on the book.

When John departed to start a doctoral program, Alex took over. Alex was, like John, an incredibly bright, creative, and talented thinker (and writer). He did a great job of helping us make sense of the reviews we got on the first draft of the book, and of listening to my ideas about how to further develop it. We needed more of a grounding in the experience of the people we wanted to read the book, to give it something of everyday life so it wouldn't be just my summaries of the musings of a bunch of dead philosophers. To make it more relevant and accessible, John and I did some initial interviews with former students to try to ground the book in the experiences and ideas of my students. Alex and I tried again, this time with less structure to the interviews and more focus on the students and their life stories. This turn proved very helpful not only for the quality of the interviews but for reimagining how we would combine the pieces of the book: starting with our everyday experience and revealing how the questions are already part of our daily lives. I wanted to help people realize how practical the questions are as a way to approach life and to pay more attention to the things we seem to go out of our way not to notice. This is a practical book, a kind of user's manual for life—even if the manual is about things to pay attention to rather than answers or instructions. It is a book about noticing.

I'm extremely grateful to both John and Alex for all they did to make this book a reality—and something much closer to the book I set out to write.

I want to thank Steve Momper for his support of this project and believing in me. It is a privilege to get to publish this book with the University of Virginia Press, especially as someone who got their PhD from UVA and worked as a professor there for twenty-two years. Steve is an incredibly kind and generous person. Every time I came by his office or saw him in the hallways, he provided encouragement for the project and gratitude for my desire to publish the book through him—even when he saw us struggling (and taking longer than we expected) to get to the version of the book you have in front of you. I can't imagine a better partner for overseeing the project and helping create a book that we both wanted to see published.

Jane Haxby has done an amazing job as an editor—though she has been much more than that. From our first conversation about the project, she seemed to grasp what I was up to and why it mattered. This feeling only deepened as we had follow-up conversations and began to dig into her edits of the chapters. Most writers, especially academics, tend to bristle at suggestions from others about how to improve their writing. We know best, we are the experts, so just approve what we wrote, please! My experience couldn't have been further from this stereotype. While she made tons of suggestions about things like wording, flow, and structure, most everything she sent my way felt like a close academic colleague helping me find a better way to express my ideas—and make them more accessible to my audience. All our conversations left me more excited, more confident in what we were doing, and with a clearer view of how to (re)shape the text. I am grateful to her for her skill, for her hard work, and most of all for being a great thought partner. This book is far better because of her efforts.

I'm also grateful to Riley Steiner for a stellar copyedit and to the rest of Darden Business Publishing—Andy Dahl, Melanie Foye, Jennifer Hasher, Joseph Hearl, Elliot Leflar, Leslie Mullin, Sherry Richardson, and Charlotte Walker—for their contributions, from editorial and production advice through marketing and sales. And I thank the UVA Press, with special thanks to Eric Brandt, Jason Coleman, Joel Coggins, Ellen Satrom, Cecilia Sorochin, and Nadine Zimmerli.

Leigh Ayers is a dear friend and an incredibly talented artist. Not only was she instrumental in Cathy and I meeting—and a bridesmaid in our wedding—but she designed this book inside and out. I'm so grateful for her compassion, her artistic insights, and her ability to visually express her deep understanding of the content of this book. I thank Leigh for her beautiful contributions to this project and her friendship over the past many years.

I'd like to thank my colleagues, particularly in the Strategy, Ethics & Entrepreneurship (SEE) area at Darden. The ideas in this book are rooted in a decidedly human-centric way of seeing life, including how we talk and think about business. Unfortunately, this approach is more the exception than the rule in business education as well as throughout universities. Particularly through working with colleagues like Ed Freeman, Bobby Parmar, Patricia Werhane, Saras Sarasvathy, and Sankaran Venkataraman (as well as the rest of my colleagues in SEE), I have found incredible support for my ideas as well as help in shaping them into versions that are not only more publishable, but richer and more accessible to both managers and academics. Being part of the ecosystem at Darden and having the audacity to think that business is about people coming together to make themselves and others better off—this is a founding inspiration for this book. I am grateful to these colleagues for their support and for all they do to develop more thoughtful and humane leaders; and especially for how they embraced me, made me feel welcome, and supported my work and my life over all these years.

And finally, this book would not exist without the students who had the curiosity and courage to take the "Ultimate Questions" course with me. This course was a dream of mine, and I am grateful to them, not only for showing up and doing the work, but for stepping into the conversations, being willing to talk about hard things with their peers, and opening up space for everyone to learn. I'd like to think that I deserve credit for the richness of the conversations and the power of the learnings, but most of that credit belongs to my students. They were the ones who decided to take on these questions, do the readings, create salon-group work, and be willing to "go there" on some really challenging topics. What ensued was the most rewarding teaching experience of my career. It was a privilege to be in the room and part of those conversations. This book is an effort to share the ideas and experiences of this course with a wider audience so they can access at least some of what my students created with each other.

NOTES

INTRODUCTION

1 For more on this change, see Patricia H. Werhane, *Adam Smith and His Legacy for Modern Capitalism* (Oxford University Press, 1991); Amartya Sen's work, especially his books *Development as Freedom* (Anchor, 2000) and *The Idea of Justice* (Belknap Press, 2011); and Dierdre McCloskey's work, especially her book *Bettering Humanomics: A New, and Old, Approach to Economic Science* (University of Chicago Press, 2021).

2 Andrew C. Wicks and R. Edward Freeman, "Organization Studies and the New Pragmatism: Positivism, Anti-Positivism, and the Search for Ethics," *Organization Science* 9, no. 2 (1998): 123–40; Andrew C. Wicks, Shawn L. Berman, and Thomas M. Jones, "The Structure of Optimal Trust: Moral and Strategic Implications," *Academy of Management Review* 24, no. 1 (1999): 99–116.

3 Robert H. Frank, *Passions Within Reason: The Strategic Role of Emotions* (Norton, 1988), cited in Wicks and Freeman, "Organization Studies and the New Pragmatism," 134.

4 Adam Smith, *The Theory of Moral Sentiments*, ed. Knud Haakonssen (Cambridge University Press, 2002), 11.

5 See, for example, R. Edward Freeman, Jeffrey S. Harrison, Andrew C. Wicks, Bidhan L. Parmar, and Simone de Colle, *Stakeholder Theory: The State of the Art* (Cambridge University Press, 2010). For reflections on the theory in late 2024, see R. Edward Freeman, "With Stakeholder Capitalism Pioneers Schwab, Dimon, and Fink Nearing Retirement, Who Will Carry the Torch Forward?," *Fortune*, November 26, 2024, https://fortune.com/2024/11/26/stakeholder-capitalism-pioneers-schwab-dimon-fink-nearing-retirement-leadership/?abc123.

6 Bidhan L. Parmar, Adrian Keevil, and Andrew C. Wicks, "People and Profits: The Impact of Corporate Objectives on Employees' Need Satisfaction at Work," *Journal of Business Ethics* 154, no. 1 (January 2019): 13–33.

7 James H. Gilmore and B. Joseph Pine II, "The Four Faces of Mass Customization," *Harvard Business Review*, January–February 1997, https://hbr.org/1997/01/the-four-faces-of-mass-customization.

CHAPTER 1. Who Are We, and Who Am I?

1 Genesis 1:27–29.

2 Galen Guengerich, "You Are the Center of the Universe: Alan Watts on How You Are the Focus of the World That Makes You Possible," *Psychology Today*, August 24, 2014, https://www.psychologytoday.com/us/blog/the-search-meaning/201408/you-are-the-center-the-universe.

3 Hannah Arendt, *The Origins of Totalitarianism* (Mariner Books Classics, 1973); Sun Tzu, *The Art of War*, trans. Thomas Cleary (Shambhala, 1988); A. M. Turing, "Computing Machinery and Intelligence," *Mind* 49 (1950): 433–60, https://courses.cs.umbc.edu/471/papers/turing.pdf.

4 Joseph Campbell, *The Hero with a Thousand Faces*, 3rd ed. (New World Library, 2008).

5 For a brief survey, see Andrew C. Wicks, Shawn L. Berman, and Thomas M. Jones, "The Structure of Optimal Trust: Moral and Strategic Implications," *Academy of Management Review* 24, no. 1 (1999): 99–116. For a good foil, see Oliver E. Williamson, "Transaction Cost Economics: The Natural Progression," Nobel Prize Lecture, December 8, 2009, https://www.nobelprize.org/uploads/2018/06/williamson_lecture.pdf.

6 See, for example, Elinor Ostrom, "Beyond Markets and States: Polycentric Governance of Complex Economic Systems," Nobel Prize lecture, December 8, 2009, https://www.nobelprize.org/uploads/2018/06/ostrom_lecture.pdf.

7 See, for example, Frans B. M. de Waal, "The Chimpanzee's Service Economy: Evidence for Cognition-Based Reciprocal Exchange," in *Trust and Reciprocity: Interdisciplinary Lessons from Experimental Research*, ed. Elinor Ostrom and James Walker, vol. VI in the Russell Sage Foundation Series on Trust (Russell Sage Foundation, 2003).

8 Kat McGowan, "Cooperation Is What Makes Us Human," *Nautilus*, April 22, 2013, https://nautil.us/cooperation-is-what-makes-us-human-rd-234316/.

9 Paul J. Zak and Stephen Knack, "Trust and Growth," working paper (Department of Economics, Claremont Graduate University, 1998).

10 Kenneth Arrow, *The Limits of Organization* (W. W. Norton & Company, 1974).

11 See, for example, Yuval Noah Harari, *Sapiens: A Brief History of Humankind* (Harper, 2015); and Joshua Greene, *Moral Tribes: Emotion, Reason, and the Gap Between Us and Them* (Penguin Press, 2013).

12 See, for example, Steven Pinker, *The Language Instinct: How the Mind Creates Language* (Harper Perennial Modern Classics, 2007); Noam Chomsky, *Language and Mind*, 3rd ed. (Cambridge University Press, 2006); Ludwig Wittgenstein, *Philosophical Investigations*, trans. G. E. M. Anscombe (Basil Blackwell Ltd, 1958).

13 Harari, *Sapiens*.

14 Soraj Hongladarom, "What Buddhism Can Do for AI Ethics," *MIT Technology Review*, January 6, 2021, https://www.technologyreview.com/2021/01/06/1015779/what-buddhism-can-do-ai-ethics/.

15 Robin Dunbar, "Dunbar's Number: Why the Theory That Humans Can Only Maintain 150 Friendships Has Withstood 30 Years of Scrutiny," Neuroscience News, August 28, 2021, https://neurosciencenews.com/dunbars-number-social-brain-19210/; Jenny Gross, "Can You Have More Than 150 Friends?," *New York Times*, May 11, 2021, https://www.nytimes.com/2021/05/11/science/dunbars-number-debunked.html.

16 Harari, *Sapiens*, 28–29.

17 Harari, *Sapiens*, 35–36.

18 "Big Five Personality Test," Open-Source Psychometrics Project, https://openpsychometrics.org/tests/IPIP-BFFM/; the Myers-Briggs Company, https://www.themyersbriggs.com/.

19 Ancestry, https://www.ancestry.com/.

20 Karen Weintraub, "The Map of Our DNA Is Finally Complete. Here's What That Means for Humanity," *USA Today*, March 31, 2022, https://www.usatoday.com/story/news/health/2022/03/31/human-genome-dna-mapping-complete/7229428001/. See also "The Human Genome Project," National Institutes of Health, https://www.genome.gov/human-genome-project.

21 Emma Goldberg, "The $2 Billion Question of Who You Are at Work," *New York Times*, March 5, 2023, https://www.nytimes.com/2023/03/05/business/remote-work-personality-tests.html.

22 The Enneagram Institute, https://www.enneagraminstitute.com/.

23 William James, *Principles of Psychology* (Dover Publications, 1950), 488.

24 James, *Principles of Psychology*, 239.

25 Laura Morgan Roberts, Gretchen M. Spreitzer, Jane E. Dutton, Robert E. Quinn, Emily Heaphy, and Brianna Barker Caza, "How to Play to Your Strengths," *Harvard Business Review*, January 2005, https://hbr.org/2005/01/how-to-play-to-your-strengths; Laura Morgan Roberts, Emily Heaphy, and Brianna Barker Caza, "To Become Your Best Self, Study Your Successes," *Harvard Business Review*, May 14, 2019, https://hbr.org/2019/05/to-become-your-best-self-study-your-successes. See also "Reflected Best Self Exercise," Michigan Ross Center for Positive Organizations, University of Michigan, https://reflectedbestselfexercise.com/.

26 Roberts, Heaphy, and Caza, "To Become Your Best Self, Study Your Successes."

CHAPTER 2. Why Are We Here, and Why Am I Here?

1 Yuval Noah Harari, *Sapiens: A Brief History of Humankind* (Harper, 2015), 25–26.

2 "Legend of the Cedar Tree," Forest History Society, https://foresthistory.org/education/trees-talk-curriculum/american-prehistory-8000-years-of-forest-management/legend-of-the-cedar-tree/.

3 "Bodh Gaya—Place of Enlightement," BuddhaNet, https://www.buddhanet.net/e-learning/buddhistworld/bodgaya/.

4 Neil Price, *Children of Ash and Elm: A History of the Vikings* (Basic Books, 2022), 36, 38.
5 San, "Iusaaset, Goddess of the Tree of Life," Iseum Sanctuary, February 14, 2022, https://iseumsanctuary.com/2022/02/14/goddess-of-the-tree-of-life/.
6 Genesis 2:17–3:19.
7 Jeanne Dorin McDowell, "The Surprising Way That Millions of New Trees Could Transform America," *National Geographic*, October 9, 2023, https://www.nationalgeographic.com/environment/article/tree-planting-american-cities-health-environment-benefits.
8 Suzanne Simard, *Finding the Mother Tree: Discovering the Wisdom of the Forest* (Vintage, 2022), 4.
9 Martin Buber, *I and Thou*, trans. Walter Kaufmann (Charles Scribner's Sons, 1970), 57–60.
10 Viktor E. Frankl, *Man's Search for Meaning*, trans. Ilse Lasch (Beacon Press, 2006), 76.
11 "Chadwick Boseman's Howard University 2018 Commencement Speech," posted May 14, 2018, by Howard University, YouTube, 34 min., 40 sec., https://www.youtube.com/watch?v=RIHZypMyQ2s, at 31:38.
12 Frankl, *Man's Search for Meaning*, 111.
13 Parissa J. Ballard, Stephanie S. Daniel, Grace Anderson, Linda Nicolotti, Elimarie Caballero Quinones, Min Lee, and Aubry N. Koehler, "Incorporating Volunteering into Treatment for Depression Among Adolescents: Developmental and Clinical Considerations," *Frontiers in Psychology* 12 (2021), https://pmc.ncbi.nlm.nih.gov/articles/PMC8131855/; Eric S. Kim, Victor J. Strecher, and Carol D. Ryff, "Purpose in Life and Use of Preventive Health Care Services," *Proceedings of the National Academy of Sciences* 111, no. 46 (2014): 16, 331–36, https://doi.org/10.1073/pnas.1414826111; Stacey M. Schaefer, Jennifer Morozink Boylan, Carien M. van Reekum, Regina C. Lapate, Catherine J. Norris, Carol D. Ryff, and Richard J. Davidson, "Purpose in Life Predicts Better Emotional Recovery from Negative Stimuli," *PLoS One* 8, no. 11 (2013): e80329, https://pmc.ncbi.nlm.nih.gov/articles/PMC3827458/; Naina Dhingra, Jonathan Emmett, Andrew Samo, and Bill Schaninger, "Igniting Individual Purpose in Times of Crisis," *McKinsey Quarterly*, August 18, 2020, https://www.mckinsey.com/capabilities/people-and-organizational-performance/our-insights/igniting-individual-purpose-in-times-of-crisis.
14 Michael Tomasello, *Why We Cooperate* (MIT Press, 2009), 9–10; see also, for example, Charlotte Nickerson, "Extrinsic vs. Intrinsic Motivation: What's the Difference?," Simply Psychology, updated September 29, 2023, https://www.simplypsychology.org/differences-between-extrinsic-and-intrinsic-motivation.html.
15 Mihaly Csikszentmihalyi, "Flow," in *Flow and the Foundations of Positive Psychology: The Collected Works of Mihaly Csikszentmihalyi* (Springer, 2014), 227 and 230.

16 See, for example, Joseph Campbell, *The Hero with a Thousand Faces*, 3rd ed. (New World Library, 2008).

17 For some perspectives on (and evidence for) creating purpose, see Campbell, *The Hero with a Thousand Faces*, as well as Patrick L. Hill, Rachel Sumner, and Anthony L. Burrow, "Understanding the Pathways to Purpose: Examining Personality and Well-Being Correlates Across Adulthood," *Journal of Positive Psychology* 9, no. 3 (2014): 227–34, https://doi.org/10.1080/17439760.2014.888584; Olga Stavrova and Maike Luhmann, "Social Connectedness as a Source and Consequence of Meaning in Life," *Journal of Positive Psychology* 11, no. 5 (2016): 470–79, https://doi.org/10.1080/17439760.2015.1117127; and Jo Ann A. Abe, "A Longitudinal Follow-Up Study of Happiness and Meaning-Making," *Journal of Positive Psychology* 11, no. 5 (2016): 489–98, https://doi.org/10.1080/17439760.2015.1117129.

18 Bidhan (Bobby) L. Parmar, Andrew C. Wicks, and R. Edward Freeman, "Stakeholder Management & The Value of Human-Centred Corporate Objectives," *Journal of Management Studies* 59, no. 2 (2022): 569–82, https://doi.org/10.1111/joms.12716.

19 Vanessa C. Burbano, Olle Folke, Stephan Meier, and Johanna Rickne, "The Gender Gap in Meaningful Work," *Management Science* 70, no. 10 (2024): 7,004–23, https://pubsonline.informs.org/doi/epdf/10.1287/mnsc.2022.01807.

20 Somini Sengupta, "How Greenwashing Fools Us," *New York Times*, August 23, 2022, https://www.nytimes.com/2022/08/23/climate/climate-greenwashing.html.

21 Arne Gast, Nina Probst, and Bruce Simpson, "Purpose, Not Platitudes: A Personal Challenge for Top Executives," *McKinsey Quarterly*, December 3, 2020, https://www.mckinsey.com/capabilities/people-and-organizational-performance/our-insights/purpose-not-platitudes-a-personal-challenge-for-top-executives; Thomas Donaldson, "Values in Tension: Ethics Away from Home," *Harvard Business Review*, September–October 1996, https://hbr.org/1996/09/values-in-tension-ethics-away-from-home.

22 Larry Fink, "Purpose and Profit: Larry Fink's 2019 Letter to CEOs," BlackRock, 2019, https://www.blackrock.com/corporate/investor-relations/2019-larry-fink-ceo-letter.

23 Dhingra, Emmett, Samo, and Schaninger, "Igniting Individual Purpose."

24 See, for example, Michael Walzer, *Thick and Thin: Moral Argument at Home and Abroad* (Notre Dame Press, 1994).

25 Parmar, Wicks, and Freeman, "Human-Centred Corporate Objectives."

26 Nickerson, "Extrinsic vs. Intrinsic Motivation."

27 Catherine Clifford, "Top Wharton Professor Adam Grant: How You Can Find Meaning in Your Work Life," CNBC, May 2, 2018, https://www.cnbc.com/2018/05/02/wharton-professor-adam-grant-how-to-find-purpose-at-work.html.

CHAPTER 3. What Is the Good Life, and What Is My Good Life?

1 Penny Locaso, "What You Were Taught About 'Happiness' Isn't True," *Harvard Business Review*, January 12, 2021, https://hbr.org/2021/01/what-you-were-taught-about-happiness-isnt-true.

2 For more on the power of regret, see Daniel H. Pink, *The Power of Regret: How Looking Backward Moves Us Forward* (Riverhead Books, 2022).

3 Martin Buber, *I and Thou*, trans. Walter Kaufmann (Charles Scribner's Sons, 1970), 57.

4 Aristotle, *The Nicomachean Ethics*, rev. ed., ed. W. D. Ross and Lesley Brown (Oxford University Press, 2009), online at https://doi.org/10.1093/actrade/9780199213610.book.1, book 1.

5 Jeremy Bentham, *Utilitarianism* (Progressive Publishing Company, 1890); John Stuart Mill, *Utilitarianism* (Parker, Son, and Bourn, 1863).

6 Viktor E. Frankl, *Man's Search for Meaning*, trans. Ilse Lasch (Beacon Press, 2006), 137.

7 Martin E. P. Seligman, *Flourish* (Free Press, 2011), 16–20. See also Positive Psychology, https://positivepsychology.com.

8 "The Top 5 Regrets of the Dying," *HuffPost*, August 3, 2013, https://www.huffpost.com/entry/top-5-regrets-of-the-dying_n_3640593.

9 "The Five Principles of Effectuation," Effectuation, https://effectuation.org/the-five-principles-of-effectuation. See also, among her many publications, Saras D. Sarasvathy, *Effectuation: Elements of Entrepreneurial Expertise*, 2nd ed. (Edward Elgar Publishing, 2022).

10 David Brooks, "To Be Happy, Marriage Matters More Than Career," *New York Times*, August 17, 2023, https://www.nytimes.com/2023/08/17/opinion/marriage-happiness-career.html.

11 Seligman, *Flourish*, 223.

12 Clayton M. Christensen, "How Will You Measure Your Life?," *Harvard Business Review*, July–August 2010, https://hbr.org/2010/07/how-will-you-measure-your-life.

13 Robert Greenleaf coined the term *servant leadership*; see, among his other work, *Servant Leadership: A Journey into the Nature of Legitimate Power and Greatness*, 25th anniversary ed. (Paulist Press, 2002).

14 Adam Grant, "In the Company of Givers and Takers," *Harvard Business Review*, April 2013, https://hbr.org/2013/04/in-the-company-of-givers-and-takers.

15 See, for example, Priya J. Wickramaratne, Tenzin Yangchen, Lauren Lepow, et al., "Social Connectedness as a Determinant of Mental Health: A Scoping Review," *PLoS One* 17, no. 10 (2022): e0275004, https://journals.plos.org/plosone/article?id=10.1371/journal.pone.0275004; Austin Perlmutter, "The Brain Benefits of Social Connection," *Psychology Today*, March 24, 2023, https://www.psychologytoday.com/us/blog/the-modern-brain/202303/the-brain-benefits-of-social-connection; and Lara B. Aknin and Ashley B.

Whillans, "Helping and Happiness: A Review and Guide for Public Policy," *Social Issues and Policy Review* 15, no. 1 (2021): 3–34, https://doi.org/10.1111/sipr.12069.

16 Brigid Schulte, "Work-Life Balance: You Can Be a Great Leader and Also Have a Life," *Harvard Business Review*, December 18, 2018, https://hbr.org/2018/12/you-can-be-a-great-leader-and-also-have-a-life.

17 Christensen, "How Will You Measure Your Life?"

18 Locaso, "What You Were Taught About 'Happiness' Isn't True."

CHAPTER 4. How Should I Get Along with Others?

1 Martin E. P. Seligman, *Flourish* (Free Press, 2011), 20.

2 Michael Tomasello, *Why We Cooperate* (MIT Press, 2009), 94.

3 Tomasello, *Why We Cooperate*, 44.

4 See, for example, Martha C. Nussbaum, "Reports from the Slaughterhouse," *New York Review of Books*, December 19, 2024, https://www.nybooks.com/articles/2024/12/19/reports-from-the-slaughterhouse-fear-factories-scully/.

5 See, for example, Sean Cummings, "Study Finds Human-Driven Mass Extinction Is Eliminating Entire Branches of the Tree of Life," *Stanford Report*, September 18, 2023, https://news.stanford.edu/stories/2023/09/human-driven-mass-extinction-eliminating-entire-genera; and "Species Extinction Rate Hundreds of Times Higher Than in Past 10 Million Years, Warns Secretary-General Observance Message, Urging Action to End Biodiversity Loss by 2030," United Nations press release, May 22, 2022, https://press.un.org/en/2022/sgsm21291.doc.htm.

6 Peter Singer, *Animal Liberation Now* (Harper, 2023), reviewed in Kelefa Sanneh, "How Far Should We Carry the Logic of the Animal-Rights Movement?," *New Yorker*, April 29, 2024, https://www.newyorker.com/magazine/2024/05/06/how-far-should-we-carry-the-logic-of-the-animal-rights-movement.

7 David Grimm, "What Are Farm Animals Thinking?," *Science*, December 7, 2023, https://www.science.org/content/article/not-dumb-creatures-livestock-surprise-scientists-their-complex-emotional-minds.

8 Peter Godfrey-Smith, "The Mind of an Octopus," *Scientific American*, January 1, 2017, https://www.scientificamerican.com/article/the-mind-of-an-octopus/.

9 Gennaro Tomma, "When They Hear Plants Crying, Moths Make a Decision," *New York Times*, December 6, 2024, https://www.nytimes.com/2024/12/06/science/moths-hearing-plant-sounds.html; Suzanne Simard, *Finding the Mother Tree: Discovering the Wisdom of the Forest* (Vintage, 2022); Kathryn Flynn, "The Idea That Trees Talk to Cooperate Is Misleading," *Scientific American*, July 19, 2021, https://www.scientificamerican.com/article/the-idea-that-trees-talk-to-cooperate-is-misleading/.

10 Yuval Harari, Tristan Harris, and Aza Raskin, "You Can Have the Blue Pill or the Red Pill, and We're Out of Blue Pills," *New York Times*, March 24, 2023, https://www.nytimes.com/2023/03/24/opinion/yuval-harari-ai-chatgpt.html; David Gunkel, "2020: The Year of Robot Rights," MIT Press Reader, January 27, 2020, https://thereader.mitpress.mit.edu/2020-the-year-of-robot-rights/; John Searle, "Consciousness in Artificial Intelligence," posted December 3, 2015, by Talks at Google, YouTube, 1 hr., 10 min., 37 sec., https://www.youtube.com/watch?v=rHKwIYsPXLg.

11 "11. Americans' Feelings About Politics, Polarization and the Tone of Political Discourse," Pew Research Center, September 19, 2023, https://www.pewresearch.org/politics/2023/09/19/americans-feelings-about-politics-polarization-and-the-tone-of-political-discourse/; Andrew Daniller, "Americans See Little Bipartisan Common Ground, but More on Foreign Policy Than on Abortion, Guns," Pew Research Center, June 25, 2024, https://www.pewresearch.org/short-reads/2024/06/25/americans-see-little-bipartisan-common-ground-but-more-on-foreign-policy-than-on-abortion-guns/.

12 Luke 10:29–37.

13 Francis Fukuyama, *The End of History and the Last Man* (Free Press, 1992).

14 Charlie Huntington, "The Milgram Experiment: Theory, Results, & Ethical Issues," Berkeley Well-Being Institute, https://www.berkeleywellbeing.com/milgram-experiment.html.

15 "The Stanford Prison Experiment," Zimbardo, https://www.zimbardo.com/the-stanford-prison-experiment/.

16 See, for example, Gina Perry, "Deception and Illusion in Milgram's Accounts of the Obedience Experiments," *Theoretical & Applied Ethics* 2, no. 2 (2013): 79–92; Thibault Le Texier, "Debunking the Stanford Prison Experiment," *American Psychologist* 74, no. 7 (2019): 823–39.

17 Leor Zmigrod, "A Neurocognitive Model of Ideological Thinking," *Politics and the Life Sciences* 40, no. 2 (2021): 224–38, https://doi.org/10.1017/pls.2021.10.

18 Malcolm Gladwell, *Talking to Strangers: What We Should Know About the People We Don't Know*, large print ed. (Little, Brown and Company, 2019), 123–26.

19 Richard Dawkins, *The Selfish Gene*, 40th anniversary ed. (Oxford University Press, 2016), 4.

20 Yuval Noah Harari, *Sapiens: A Brief History of Humankind* (Harper, 2015), 29–30.

21 Martin Buber, *I and Thou*, trans. Walter Kaufmann (Charles Scribner's Sons, 1970), 103.

22 Aristotle, *The Nicomachean Ethics*, rev. ed., ed. W. D. Ross and Lesley Brown (Oxford University Press, 2009), online at https://doi.org/10.1093/actrade/9780199213610.book.1, book 1, 4 (1094b).

23 Jeremy Bentham, *Utilitarianism* (Progressive Publishing Company, 1890), 12–13.

24 Bidhan L. Parmar, Adrian Keevil, and Andrew C. Wicks, "People and Profits: The Impact of Corporate Objectives on Employees' Need Satisfaction at Work," *Journal of Business Ethics* 154, no. 1 (January 2019): 17. See also Mary Sully de Luque, Nathan Washburn, David Waldman, and Robert J. House, "Unrequited Profit: How Stakeholder and Economic Values Relate to Subordinates' Perceptions of Leadership and Firm Performance," *Administrative Science Quarterly* 53, no. 4 (2008): 626–54.

25 Bidhan (Bobby) L. Parmar, Andrew C. Wicks, and R. Edward Freeman, "Stakeholder Management & The Value of Human-Centred Corporate Objectives," *Journal of Management Studies* 59, no. 2 (2022): 569–82, https://doi.org/10.1111/joms.12716. See also Varda Liberman, Steven M. Samuels, and Lee Ross, "The Name of the Game: Predictive Power of Reputations Versus Situational Labels in Determining Prisoner's Dilemma Game Moves," *Personality and Social Psychology Bulletin* 30, no. 9 (2004): 1,175–85.

26 Thomas Donaldson, "Values in Tension: Ethics Away from Home," *Harvard Business Review*, September–October 1996, https://hbr.org/1996/09/values-in-tension-ethics-away-from-home.

27 Seligman, *Flourish*, 20.

APPENDIX 1. A Guide to Having Hard Conversations

1 Stuart M. Matlins and Arthur J. Magida, eds., *How to Be a Perfect Stranger: The Essential Religious Etiquette Handbook*, 6th ed. (SkyLight Paths Publishing, 2015).

INDEX

ABOUT THE AUTHORS

Andrew C. Wicks is the Ruffin Professor of Business Administration and Richard M. Waitzer Bicentennial Professor of Ethics at the University of Virginia Darden School of Business.

He has served on the UVA faculty since 2002 and in leadership roles including director of the Olsson Center for Applied Ethics, academic director of the Institute for Business in Society, academic adviser for the Business Roundtable Institute for Corporate Ethics, and director of Darden's doctoral program. He has taught in numerous MBA and executive education programs throughout his years at Darden, including custom programs and direct consulting with a variety of companies. He also served as an adjunct professor in UVA's Department of Religious Studies and the Frank Batten School of Leadership and Public Policy, and he has regularly taught abroad.

Wicks has published over fifty articles in a wide array of peer-reviewed journals in business ethics, management, and the humanities. He has served on several editorial boards and as guest editor for several special issues. He is the author of over fifty items of teaching material and has coauthored and coedited books including *The Moral Imagination of Patricia Werhane: A Festschrift*, *Public Trust in Business*, *Stakeholder Theory: The State of the Art*, *Managing for Stakeholders: Survival, Reputation, and Success*, and *Business Ethics: A Managerial Approach*. He has received numerous awards for both his research and teaching and has been quoted in mainstream media such as *Bloomberg Businessweek*, *Financial Times*, *Fortune*, NPR, and *The Washington Post*.

Through his teaching and research, Wicks encourages us to ask questions about how we live and operate in the world—as individuals, as organizations, and as a society. He examines topics such as trust, managerial mindset, value pluralism and accountability, health care ethics, total quality management, and stakeholder theory as it relates to morality and spirituality. His primary focus in his research and teaching is on human beings and human welfare in the context of business, particularly through the lens of stakeholder theory. This book grew out of his desire to make widely available the opportunities for rich exploration and hard conversations he and his students found in the class he designed, "Ultimate Questions and Creating Value for Stakeholders."

He continues to enjoy out-of-doors activities, music, art, and all things Tennessee Volunteers, as well as conversations with family, friends, and students. He and his wife Cathy have returned to the mountains of Colorado with their dog Sam.

Alexander S. Bleiberg is pursuing a master's degree in counseling at the Institute for Clinical Social Work. He was a doctoral candidate in politics at the University of Virginia, where he was Andrew Wicks's research assistant. He studied qualitative methods at the Institute for Qualitative and Multi-Method Research, was an editorial and research assistant at University College London in the department of psychoanalysis, and earned a master's degree in social science from the University of Chicago. He has also worked as a procurement analyst at Great Dane Trailers. He enjoys learning about black holes, reading novels about misfits, and drinking lemon ginger tea.

John K. Nolan was a research assistant for Andrew Wicks and is the coauthor of four business ethics cases. He is currently a PhD candidate in divinity at the University of Aberdeen.

DARDEN BUSINESS BOOKS, an imprint of the University of Virginia Press, aims to improve the world by publishing thought-leading works in business and economics that will inspire responsible leaders. In support of this mission, Darden Business Books recruits authors from varied backgrounds and fields to provide diverse perspectives and a wide range of ideas, helps them refine and effectively communicate their scholarship and expertise, and distributes their work to the widest audience possible.